A YEAR OF STILLNESS

ALSO BY JUSSI NIITTYVIITA

We Were Once Human

Seeker of Silences

I Forgive You

A YEAR OF STILLNESS

JUSSI NIITTYVIITA

 SEEKER OF SILENCES

ISBN 978-952-69223-6-2 (hardback)
ISBN 978-952-69223-2-4 (paperback)
ISBN 978-952-69223-3-1 (eBook)

To the mind that is still, the whole universe surrenders.

Lao Tzu

CONTENTS

THE MEANING OF THIS BOOK

A silent and soothing stillness breathes within you. Whenever the stillness inhales, some beautiful state accompanies it; unconditional joy, deep feelings of love, recognition of intense beauty, inner peace and compassion, and many others. When the stillness exhales, those beautiful states extend outward from you, propelling peace and compassion into the world around you.

In the many paths of your life, you have undoubtedly experienced such beautiful states, regardless of what kind of life has happened for you. These beautiful states are already present in you, and they arise from the stillness that breathes within us all. And how do I know this? Because I am just like you—imperfect in many ways and trying to acquire peace in my own terms.

Acquiring peace is much simpler than it seems. Being at peace does not require anything of you. Only your thoughts require something of you, and this is why you mostly don't feel at peace. Most often, the stillness within you is overlooked and obscured by your cherished ability of thinking—your mind is full of illusions and it speaks so loudly that you cannot hear yourself. Don't get drawn into those illusions, but simply seek to become aware of them. Someone wise once said:

Looking straight at illusions will shatter them.

Following this wisdom is what produced the book you now hold in your hands. *A Year of Stillness* describes a year in ordinary human life with its ups and downs. At first glance, it might seem that life is a pendulum swinging between peace and chaos, but ultimately, it becomes evident that chaos is merely another illusion. If, however, chaos feels more familiar to you at the moment—and inner peace seems a distant thought in your world—just remind yourself that you already bear within you stillness and peace. It is not that you do not have those experiences; it is just a matter of awareness. Pure and unjudging awareness of anything changes *everything*.

You deserve to find yourself in the myriad pathways of the world, and when you do, you will know peace. You do not have to become anything to find yourself. You need only be still and know that you *are*. Welcome to *A Year of Stillness*.

Kuivaniemi, Finland
25th of June 2019
Jussi Niittyviita

JANUARY

1ˢᵗ OF JANUARY

The first day of a new year dawns in soothing darkness. A sense of peace is present. A fascinating and sacred silence embraces the moment. The stillness within is beautiful, and the peace remains, even when noisy children are playing and running around. They occasionally argue and need their parents' attention, but even that does not disturb the peace experienced today. Only a subtle pull towards thinking happens at times, but the thoughts fade away quickly, just like the breath evaporates into the surrounding cold air.

The darkness of the winter is impenetrable. The sun barely rises at all during the day. However, there is something very serene in the dark embrace of mother nature. The absence of natural light somehow creates space for the absence of thoughts, in the same way as the absence of noise allows silence to emerge.

Fresh snow covers the ground. Seawater seeps through the layer of thin ice just a few meters away from the waterfront. Yesterday it was all just immovable ice, and most likely it will be so again tomorrow when the air grows colder. The change in nature happens with a curious and inexorable certainty. Occasionally, the mind tries to contemplate that change, but thinking about nature's phenomena does not seem to add any real value to the pure experiences of those phenomena. Thinking always includes added value that is created apparently out of thin air. A subtle and untouchable peace lies in the silence of the mind, but the compulsion to think creates a veil in front of that peace. All value that is created through thinking can be justified only through more thinking. Is there any real value in thoughts that only symbolize other thoughts? Such is the problem of the human mind.

What would be a more promising start for a new year than to remain the first day in an undefinable state of inner stillness? In that stillness, a new and deeper dimension of life is revealed.

2ᴺᴰ OF JANUARY

Driving to work for the first time this year. Short glimpses of the peace experienced yesterday appear in the mind, but they are only memories. They are not the experience.

Thoughts try to reach for the peace, but only the reaching happens.

The mind tries to find value in the present moment by forcing the peace to come back. It has created a shining trophy of the inner stillness described by the memories of yesterday. The mind cannot understand that inner peace never comes by applying force. The peace within any moment is revealed only in the natural flow of the world—not in the efforts of trying to control that flow.

The traffic of the morning hours is intense. The headlights of numerous cars are flowing like an endless river of spherical lights in the surrounding darkness. Suddenly, amid the heavy traffic, it unfolds again—*the stillness*. A curious feeling always arises when the stillness reveals itself because it includes a total cessation of thoughts. It always occurs without warning, without a personal investment of making it happen. After a while of just dwelling in inner stillness, the mind draws memories of the younger daughter exclaiming after a recent birthday party: "It is so silent here. So silent. Children are very noisy." She herself is most of the time very noisy, and maybe that is why she notices the silences.

After repeating the memory for a while, the mind falls silent again. Everything that remains is the road, the car, the flow of headlights, and the dance of the traffic in general. There are no problems in the present moment, nothing to achieve, nowhere else to be, and nothing to resist or avoid. A distant sound of a car horn colors the continuous hum of the traffic. After that, everything is rendered to soothing background noise again.

A silent peacefulness lingers below the surface of the traffic. The mind stays quiet for a long period of time, before arriving to work. Soon after, a stream of compulsive thinking and conditioned behavioral patterns wash away the peaceful stillness.

3ᴿᴰ OF JANUARY

Trembling hands and mild sweating while presenting the results of a project to a client. It is strange because there seems to be no stress involved in the situation. The mind feels confident, and the client is most certainly satisfied. Nevertheless, the mind does not like the idea of stress in the situation, and maybe that is why the symptoms of stress occur. The body acts in the most simple ways when attention is given to its functions.

While speaking and listening in turn, the attention is getting pulled elsewhere. Fortunately, the client and colleagues do not seem to notice the light distraction. An illusion of participation is created in an apparently convincing way. The snowflakes slowly fall on the people walking in the street, and they pull the awareness like a magnet. Everyone seems to be in a hurry, for whatever reasons they harbor within. Many of them walk with blind eyes, sunken into the deep waters of their thoughts. Only a few seem to really notice the beautiful snowfall, even though every one of them is walking through and in it.

What would be more important at that particular moment? Thoughts? Personal problems? A sense of hurry? Some more important place to be? Memories of yesterday? Mental images of tomorrow?

Attention is empowerment in its purest form. It flows like a vast river through the kingdoms of acceptance and resistance. Ultimately, acceptance is the only kingdom there is. Everything is always rendered to acceptance, but usually, it happens through resistance, through mostly redundant thinking. The mind that blinds the people from seeing the subtle beauty of the snowfall is a sophisticated mechanism of resistance.

The snow keeps on falling. The dialogue about the project results continues.

4TH OF JANUARY

Alone. The family is elsewhere for the night. The house is very silent. The mind is restless because it is not used to such silence in an environment, which usually includes sounds of children running around and playing. A recently released samurai movie colors the evening with lots of swords, blood, and gore. The mind has a fascinating habit of longing for feelings of fear and even revulsion. The movie indeed creates such feelings, but it must be seen nevertheless. It has a strange gravity in it, and there is no use in resisting that gravity.

The mind races after watching the movie. The scenes of blood and severed limbs flow in the stream of thoughts. Parts of the movie are replayed in mental images many times during the rest of the evening. Whenever strong emotions are present, the mind tends to go into repeat mode. Repetition is the tool it uses to imprint memories in the unexamined corners of the human identity.

The silence that filled the house all evening starts to feel more alive when lying in bed. The inner stillness unfolds through that silence. It happens suddenly, without any warning, as it always does. Nothing else arises in the awareness, but the warm bed, the gloomy lights of the room, the ceiling, the walls, the sound of breathing, subtle tingling in the fingers and toes, and the soft feeling of the bed under the body. No thoughts arise. The inner stillness prevails. A car drives by and the mind fills the awareness just for a fraction of a second to label the sound as a car, and then it falls silent again. The stillness is very present. Everything is immovable and yet continuously changing.

5ᵀᴴ OF JANUARY

No light exists that could cast a shadow. Light is all there is. It penetrates every single thing in consciousness, adopting myriad forms and an infinity of experiences. Whatever the actual nature of light is, it is most likely something that cannot be conveyed using words, images, or thoughts. Even to call it *light* is profoundly misleading.

A deep sacredness and austerity are felt in the way everything unfolds. Snow falls down slowly and serenely.

The dark sky spreads out to open its endless embrace over the cold ground. The temperature is just below zero degrees. The gentle coldness is perceived in the snowflakes as well. Their falling seems effortless, and the white blanket of new snow on the ground looks very soft and light.

Streetlights penetrate the snowfall to create a sharp contrast with the surrounding darkness of winter. Darkness and light are truths that conflict with each other, and can yet live with each other; shadows that are seen as shadows are essentially full of light. The strange dichotomy of light and darkness swirls in the mind, but the mind cannot grasp it. Despite the mind's best efforts, only the grasping occurs, and nothing else.

The mind falls silent again. Only the faint sound of the footsteps on the snowy ground remains. Even moving through the snowfall, everything feels very still and peaceful.

6TH OF JANUARY

The level of energy in children is sometimes incomprehensible. The new day dawns very early, and the daughters are playing and singing in their parents' bedroom. Where do they derive their energy from, especially at such early hours?

Children are apparently not burdened by a sense of identity—that would limit their energy. The inner resistance in children is mostly minimal. Whatever mishaps they experience, they tend to shrug it off quite fast.

It is a skill not many adults are capable of. Instead of moving forward, the adults usually dwell in the memories or expectations of their problematic life situations.

Emotions are empowered most efficiently when given undivided attention. This does not mean intellectually contemplating the emotions, but directly feeling them just as they are, without a single thought running through the mind. Allowing the emotions to be just as they are is witnessing creation in its purest form. Through this witnessing, changes happen; sorrow and anger might turn into joy in a blink of an eye. In the natural fluctuation of emotions, no grasping thoughts arise that would make one dwell in the achieved state of mind or emotions.

The joyous play of children usually expresses the fluctuation of emotions in perfect harmony with the surrounding world. The hurt they might occasionally feel is an expression of that same fluctuation. The only thing that breaks the perfect harmony of a child's temper tantrum is an adult who does not allow the tantrum to take place. Reason and intellect seldom have any constructive effect when dealing with strong emotions. Actually, rational thinking seems to only strengthen emotions that are already strong to begin with.

7TH OF JANUARY

The sun lights up the open sky and sheds golden rays on the white snowy landscape. Only a few clouds are seen in the distance. Their edges are colored in the most magnificent hues which only the winter sun can bring into existence. The mind is open like the sky above, and every once in a while, only a thought or two float by. Inner peace and stillness prevail. Everything is beautiful in an effortless way, and thinking does not add anything to the situation. Any thought seems to only diminish the situation.

The children are playing in the snow. They must be advised a few times because of their rough behavior toward each other. Parents are usually blind in the way they raise their children. They tend to repeat the past and the way they have been raised themselves. Parents bestow their offspring all the worries, expectations, regrets, joys, resentments, gratitudes, pleasures, and sufferings as they harbor within themselves. They expect the children to become like themselves, but that easily inflicts more or less unnecessary suffering on the children because no human being and no child is what we think they are.

What drives another human being cannot be known entirely, no matter how much their behavior is scrutinized. Whatever one recognizes as another's thoughts is only a projection in one's own mind—a mental image of the other person. Whatever words come out of their mouths, or whatever actions they commit, are only indistinct clouds in the open sky. Judging someone for their words or actions is an act of expressing one's own ignorance.

Raising children to become like their parents is an unconscious effort in trying to raise mental images of the parents themselves. Even though there might be partial successes, it is thoroughly impossible, given the endless unexamined layers of the human mind. Therefore, any advice given to children should first go through an open awareness of the parent's own thoughts and expectations. Most pieces of advice are not necessary at all because children will inevitably grow up without the constant interfering of adults and their deeply rooted mental positions.

8TH OF JANUARY

The mind is restless today, and it drifts into deep realms of compulsive thinking. Not a moment of inner stillness arises. Only a memory of it remains, and a memory of something apparently better than this moment always creates a grain of suffering inside.

9TH OF JANUARY

The mind is restless for the whole morning, but suddenly, during lunchtime, a powerful and primordial thought appears seemingly unprompted:

There is nothing else.

The thought brings about a very profound experience that cannot be conveyed through words. Words can point to it, but even an infinite number of them can at best only symbolize the experience. There is nothing else than *what is*, and there is nothing to think or say about *what is*. For some unknown reason, the hands seek the computer and start moving—typing letters, and creating the very words written here. There is no intention driving the body and the fingers, but the writing occurs nevertheless. Everything always occurs nevertheless.

There is nothing else. The statement includes everything that is happening now in the consciousness; the room, the people, the sounds, the smells, the lights, the emotions, and even the thoughts. They are all part of it, and there is nothing else.

Reality is incredibly simple whenever thoughts cease. It is loving, but not in the conceptual and grasping way of love. Existence expresses its love in very subtle ways. It can be felt in the coldness of winter, the soles of a shoe crunching against the snowy ground, the chilling breeze in one's face, the still and white landscape, the cold snow in one's bare hands, the cool air in the lungs. It is not love that is dependent on conditions. This love has no object.

The crisp and cold air embraces the whole nature. The trees are clad in shining white frost, and their skeleton-like structures that are covered by green leaves in the summer can be clearly seen. They are very still, and the stillness soothes the mind. Whatever problems there might be—worries or regrets—that made the mind restless before are now gone. A stillness of the surrounding world remains, and *there is nothing else.*

10TH OF JANUARY

An eerie mist covers the landscape. Distant lights penetrate the wall of fog and everything seems very peaceful. The embrace of the mist, combined with the darkness of the morning and the whiteness of the ground and trees emphasize the stillness experienced within. It is not freezing, but cold enough to keep the snow in the form of snow. However, calling it the snow, or the water, or the mist, is only secondhand knowledge of the surrounding world. The primary knowledge is the direct experience of it.

The mind has a curious compulsion to freeze the surrounding world into constant and unchanging symbols. When does snow cease to be snow and turn into water? When does warmth cease to be warm and turn into coldness? It certainly has nothing to do with the temperature scales of Celsius and Fahrenheit. Any kind of scale is a symbolic representation of the changing world. Symbolic representations cannot convey the essence of the world, much like an icon of God in a church cannot convey what God actually is, or how a photograph of a person is nothing more than a lifeless representation of that person. Symbolic representations can only create images in the mind. All thoughts the mind comes up with are ephemeral, including the idea of identity. In stillness, when the mind falls silent, the natural flux of existence can be sensed, instead of turning life's happenings into solid concepts.

When there are less sensory perceptions around, like when surrounded by a dense mist, the more the mind tries to activate streams of thought. The mind triggers imaginary memories or expectations that do not bear any real connection to the present moment. If the compulsion to think in the moments of external silence can be observed, the compulsion disappears, and thinking becomes volitional. This means one does not have to think if one does not need to think. And when one does not need to think, a significant part of all suffering, anxiety, irritation, hatred, envy, jealousy, resentment, regret, or worry ceases to be. However, in what is considered a normal mental state, the coming and going of chaotic thoughts cannot be controlled.

A lack of sensory perceptions can create an opening. The darkness of the night, or the whiteness of the impenetrable mist, or the absence of sounds, can call upon the silence of the mind. Inner silence is always revealed when one becomes aware of the silence of the external world.

11TH OF JANUARY

Temper tantrums of the younger daughter make the morning feel impossible to survive. The mind holds much irritation and frustration within, and the feelings are only emphasized by the irrational waves of a child's anger and tears. No traces of inner stillness are present. Everything is colored with negative thoughts and emotions. The mind desperately seeks a way out of the situation and longs for a happier state of being. Thankfully, the older daughter meets all expectations fully and assists in handling the situation and getting to daycare.

Existence is a perfectly written book. It carries within no mistakes, and the story it tells is most fascinating. The ability to read it, however, has been suppressed by the ability to think—especially the tendency for compulsive thinking. Thinking usually points anywhere else but the naked existence of things. A significant part of life is missed when one derives a sense of identity from the thought-based entity created by the human mind. The story in the book of existence is realized only partially while dwelling in the expectations of tomorrows and the memories of yesterdays.

Typically, the young ones wait for the future to come, and the old ones look back to the past. Somewhere in the middle of all the expecting and recalling dwells the most essential part of it all. It is found in every single word in the book of life. If any word gets bypassed while reading, something essential is missed. It is not a book to be read in a hurry. The words might contain a child's tantrums and all sorts of negative emotions, or they might hold a child's carefree state of unconditional joy. If there is a desire to jump over any part of the book, to expect something to happen, or to wait for a situation to be resolved, or even to commit actions with a specific goal in mind, then only a mental image of the book is formed. It is an image that only symbolizes the life that covers everything in existence.

What would be any more perfect than the page that is open right now, the present moment?

12ᵀᴴ OF JANUARY

A wisdom tooth removal, and not the easiest one. During the operation, the mind is very still and quiet. There is some tenseness in the body amidst all the drilling and cracking of the tooth, but the body relaxes by itself when the mind stays quiet. A very subtle peace remains throughout the operation, even though every sound and sensation of it is felt. The body adapts to the conditions by tensing and relaxing in a natural flow. It seems to do whatever the situation and the surgeon's actions require it to do.

After the operation, when the local anesthesia starts to fade away, the pain begins to creep in. At first, it lingers and builds up slowly, but after a while, it grows to a magnitude of extensive unease. Very much discomfort is present. Despite a decent amount of painkillers, the pain still pushes everything else away and fills the consciousness with all its grandeur. The body feels the pain, but the mind stays quiet.

13ᵀᴴ OF JANUARY

The pain is very intense. The day holds a lot of physical discomfort.

14TH OF JANUARY

A few moments of peace arise, but not like the peace that is experienced in the silence of the mind. This peace is a result of the temporary physical relief as the pain subsides for a while. For most of the day the pain is intense, though. The ephemeral moments of peace are a fulfillment of the mind's effort to get rid of the pain. This peace is time-bound and depends entirely on whether the pain is there or not. This peace is in the realm of the mind, even though chaotic thoughts swirl around. The mind can be at peace only when it thinks it is at peace. It knows no unconditional peace.

One can never achieve true peace if the streams of thought do not cease. Today it feels impossible, and the mere striving for peace seems to push it further away.

15TH OF JANUARY

Working at home. The mind is very restless. Important things must be delivered to the client, and the pain of the tooth removal still lingers somewhere in the background. The mind wants to get rid of the pain already, but the wanting cannot make it go away. The wanting intensifies the pain and the negative feelings it inflicts on the situation. Some anxiety is felt because of an inner conflict between what is and what the mind thinks should be.

The mind needs the pain to stop. Maybe that is the reason why the aching has intensified early in the morning.

There is no sign of it subsiding today, but somewhere behind the curtain of the curious play of the body and the mind, a very subtle and almost unnoticeable stillness is experienced. The experience is so fragile that whenever one tries to grasp it, the experience vanishes. When letting the stillness be, without any attempt at keeping or even noticing it, one can see how the mind struggles.

The mind cannot accept its coerced coexistence with the body. The body does not fight against the lingering pain in the jaw because on some level it knows the pain as an attribute of itself. The mind, however, holds any kind of mental or physical pain as a deficiency or a state of lack. The separation between the mind and the body creates an inner conflict. The mind needs something else, but the body is content with whatever is. Together they form a beautiful picture in the vast mosaic of life. All life depends on myriad levels of resistance and tension between different perceptions.

The soft wind lifts up some snow from the roof of the opposite building. The snowflakes start swirling down to the white ground, eventually disappearing into the embrace of the peaceful winter. The stillness stays, even though the mind struggles.

16TH OF JANUARY

People dare not look into each other's eyes while walking the snow-covered street. Their empty eyes stare somewhere beyond the actual reality. Their faces are slightly bent towards the ground, and their steps are long. Everyone seems to be in an undefined state of hurry. Their foreheads are covered with soft wrinkles, as they are apparently submerged in their compulsive thinking patterns. As more and more people walk by, their facial expressions whisper silent words: "What is the next place I need to be in? Am I late? Did I remember everything when dropping the children off at daycare? What time do they have to be picked up? I must not be running late for that, but is there enough time to do the work today? Why must it be snowing all the time? Why must it be so slippery here? Am I there yet?"

People usually drown out the deep-rooted thinking patterns so they can forget the present moment. Most of the time, there seems to be an urge to achieve something in the future—a state of mind, or arriving at a particular time in a certain place. What is not seen in this unconscious process is that when one arrives at last, there will always be the next place to be in or a future task to do. In the realm of the mind, there is no such thing as '*already there*', and if such a state of mind exists, it is temporary at best.

Suddenly, and without any intention, the feet stop moving. Subtle heartbeats pound in the chest, and the inhalation slowly rises in the body. An effortless exhalation follows. Some snowflakes fall from the gloomy sky. The feet are firmly rooted in the ice-covered ground. The aliveness of the body feels to penetrate everything. A few faces rise to wonder the abnormality of a still and standing human being in the middle of the street, but quickly the mind engulfs the curiosity of those few again.

A small girl with a big backpack walks by, possibly going to school. She smiles, and there is something serene in her smile. No words are needed, only the smile. In human communication, the words carry significantly less power than the silence in between. Whenever attention is given to the silence, a world of deeply beautiful and yet simple things emerge.

The feet start moving again as if they have a will of their own. The inner silence remains, though the body moves.

17TH OF JANUARY

The ache of tooth removal still comes and goes, like occasional waves hitting the shores of an ocean. The lower lip and some teeth are completely numb. Is it part of the body if it cannot be felt at all? Only a mind-made image of the physical sensation that should be there, instead of the numbness, remains. It causes some psychological unease.

19TH OF JANUARY

The oneness of everything penetrates the consciousness like a blade of the present moment, which is painfully accurate in the way it drives between the images of the past and future. The experience is not called upon in any way but happens spontaneously many times throughout the day. The mind is silent, and no labeling, criticizing, judging, or comparing occurs. Despite the total and undeniable silence of the mind, one is still conscious, and extremely aware of being conscious. The mind cannot add anything to the awareness by its conceptual contemplation and continuous labeling of things. Everything the mind does seems to only diminish the actual reality.

The formless, which is seen as the many forms in the surrounding world, is also felt very intensely within. It is a oneness that has no beginning or ending, either in time or in space. Everything existent shares the sacredness of the oneness: the good and the bad, the fearful and the lovable, the old and the young, the believers and non-believers, the ugly and the beautiful, the intelligent and the unintelligent, the poor and the rich, the spiritualists and materialists. It does not judge anything as it takes all these different forms. Only when oneness forgets itself and identifies with the forms does the feeling of oneness disappear. Thus appears the perceptions of here and there, concepts of one and the other, and the judgments of right and wrong.

All separation is profoundly illusory. Opposites do not and cannot exist apart from one another. Their purpose, if there is any at all on this level of thinking, is found only in their interaction and synergy with each other. Opposites fulfill one another. Ultimately, all opposites are one. All mental positions are one. All identities and personalities are one.

The oneness feels like an invitation, not an achievement. It is not a result of personal actions in any way. There has been no striving for it today. Not even a grain of effort for reaching it. Most probably that is why the experience of oneness and pristine stillness reveals itself. Usually, a spiritual seeker's mind will create an illusion of not striving, to attain something it believes more beautiful than the present state of mind. When the illusion is followed blindly, it results in draining energy, both mentally and physically. It might not feel like energy deprivation at first, but after days or weeks or months of living in the mind-made concept of egolessness, the truth about the illusion is revealed.

Life will make everyone humble—even a spiritual seeker. It is inevitable. And through humble perception, the oneness slowly starts to fade back in.

20ᵀᴴ OF JANUARY

Everything is movement, and yet a very subtle stillness breathes in everything. The space that contains the movement of objects is essentially tranquil and still. It is unmoving. The experience of the stillness, the great unmoving, can be acquired only when observing the movement of objects. It is not brought about by any kind of an artificial sensory deprivation or a forced lack of thoughts. True meditation is not about making the mind still and temporarily peaceful. Given the nature of the mind, that is impossible. But true meditation reveals an opening, a state where the mind can be still and peaceful. There is no success or failure in such a state of being.

21ST OF JANUARY

In the afternoon, while driving to a children's birthday party, a curious change in the mind's thinking patterns is felt. It is an almost unnoticeable fissure in the identity and personal beliefs. An intense moment of presence emerges through that fissure, and the continuous voice of thinking is rendered silent instantly. Only a clear image of the last thought remains, that apparently does not arise from the mind's conditioning:

I am nothing like that.

The strange thought creates a void, an empty hole in the shell of the identity. No thoughts arise when the light of awareness shines on the section of the mind, that withheld a pattern of self-image before. Nothing is there anymore. *"I am nothing like that."* Emptiness unfolds within—an emptiness full of life and forms.

Not much time passes, only a minute or so, and a thought appears seemingly out of nowhere. Then another, and after that, more and more. The thoughts wash over the awareness like a giant wave. The mind seems to be in panic mode. The mind cannot hold emptiness within because the very existence of the identity it has created is based on becoming or doing something. Nothingness cannot be part of it. An entirely new, fresh belief is repeated in the mind: "I am like this. I was nothing like that, but now I am like this." The soothing emptiness is now filled with a sense of becoming.

The mind upholds a continuous reconstruction process of the identity. Whenever one discovers not being something, the mind starts to reconstruct a new identity from the fragments of the old one. If the process is resisted, the resistance becomes an essential part of the new identity. If the process happens without resistance, it will simply happen, whether one is aware of it or not. There is nothing that can be done to completely change the mind-made identity or to stop the incessant streams of thought. The change happens only when no force is exercised over the mind. Any force applied in order to change the mind is only an expression of the mind itself in different forms. Seeking to change the identity that already is, is not the way to liberation.

The sun shines behind a wall of fog, spreading its rays of untouched light over the wintry landscape. The identity feels whole again, but the stillness that was perceiving the whole reconstruction process stays present. The stillness within sees the mind and all thoughts that take place just as beautiful and sacred as the sun and the rays of light it sheds everywhere around. It sees everything as perfection, without any judgments at all.

24TH OF JANUARY

Sitting in the backseat of a taxi, on the way to a client meeting. Without any warning, the subtle feeling of presence spontaneously deepens in the middle of a conversation. The mystical nature of the surrounding world suddenly seems evident and amazing. The words of the conversation do not have the same meaning as just seconds ago. They are just a medium of communication between life forms. The words are perceived as vehicles for creating an interaction, and interactions would not be possible if they were not perceived from two different perspectives. Also, the traffic does not seem like traffic anymore, but as objects moving in perfect harmony with each other.

The feeling of a hurry that was creating some stress before has now disappeared. No thoughts whisper: "We're late, we must hurry, damn this traffic..." The situation remains exactly the same as minutes ago, but everything is profoundly different. There is subtle peace in everything, even in the relatively strong opinions the driver offers for the ongoing conversation. Everything is still, and yet changing.

The sky is gloomy. A snowstorm is building in intensity and thoughts regarding the possibly delayed airplane departure appear. They are repeated in the mind a few times, and then all thoughts fade away. Everything that remains is the sky, the snow, the wind, the conversation, and the traffic.

26ᵀᴴ OF JANUARY

Yesterday it was raining, and now it is freezing cold again. The ground is covered with slippery ice. All the footprints and tracks that were pressed in the soft slush yesterday are now frozen in their rugged and abstract forms.

While walking to work, the mind rages about myriad things, but suddenly a single, out of context thought appears seemingly out of nowhere. It is entirely independent of the chaotic thought patterns of the mind:

All fear is illusory.

The state of psychological fear, in which many people typically walk through their lives, is a miscreation of the mind. The thoughts describing the state of fear have very little or no connection at all to the situation one faces. Psychological fear is always an attempt of external searching, and whatever is sought from the external world, does not exist—all experiences are created within.

Fear is a state of mind, where one strives to grasp and hold on to a mental position interpreted as the identity. In other words, psychological fear is always some form of fear of death. It does not mean physical death in every situation, but the destruction of the current pattern of thoughts and beliefs, that one is identified with. The false identity always seeks to remain as it is, and if its continuity is threatened in any way, it expresses itself in fearful thoughts and emotions.

Natural stress and the urge for survival should not be mistaken for the state of psychological fear. They are two profoundly different behavioral patterns. When one can embrace pure human emotions when facing a dangerous situation, while holding the ability to discard any thoughts constructed around those emotions, one can find freedom. This freedom is nothing thoughts can describe.

Fear is an expression of compulsive thinking, and emotions are the embodiment of unconditional love. In the silence of the mind and the stillness of simply being, fear and love are in plain sight. One can eventually see that fear is a state of mind which points to something that does not exist. All fear is illusory.

29TH OF JANUARY

Hurry. An intense sensation of hurry is the driver today. Work needs to be done. Projects need to be delivered. New customers need to be lured in. Old customers must be cared for. Co-workers must be helped and instructed. Children must be taken to the dance lesson. Some papers need to be delivered to the daycare. The next day's schedule needs to be planned. A total identification with external searching goes on.

Somewhere deep within, however, a lingering sense of still presence awaits. It is occasionally felt as a remembrance, but not in the form of memory or thought. The stillness is something that one almost remembers, but when it needs to be clad in thoughts or words, nothing comes out. In its subtlest and most unnoticeable form, the inner stillness creates an aura of peace in the middle of the busiest day. One cannot be apart of it no matter how burdened with thinking one is. The mind rages about myriad things, but no suffering is present. Somehow, thoughts today do not create the negative emotions as they many times do.

30TH OF JANUARY

The deep and relentless darkness of midwinter recedes day by day. It feels nice.

31ST OF JANUARY

Even though the winter still prevails, the first harbingers of spring have appeared. The birds sing their beautiful songs early in the morning, coloring the landscape with their voices along with the distant rays of the sun. Everything seems remarkably bright, and there is a delicate freshness in the air.

The world is always fresh and new. Nature looks forward, not backward. There is nothing in the world that can be defined as *again*. Nothing happens twice, but only once. The whole existence is destroyed and created at the same time, and the destruction and creation are the same thing. The continuous wave of appearance and disappearance flows through everything, creating a curious sensation of time in the present moment. If one is led astray by the concept of time, into the past or future, the magnificent nature of the flux of the world hide behind the veil of thinking.

The present moment is the point in the ocean, where the crest becomes the trough, and the trough becomes the crest. It is where the past is being destroyed, and the future is being created simultaneously. Nothing can be apart from it. The process includes everyone and everything in existence. It embraces everything that has ever happened and will ever happen. There is nothing mystical about the process, and the experience it brings is clear as the blue sky in the extreme coldness of winter. There is nothing poetic about it, as poetry is an art of abstractions. There is nothing abstract in it because it is. The process of appearance and disappearance, creation and destruction, is uncaused in the forever renewing present moment. The present moment has nothing to do with concepts of time. The essence of it is timeless.

The present moment holds nothing within that can be reached, gained, sought, or solved. It is beautiful.

FEBRUARY

1ˢᵀ OF FEBRUARY

A yearning to know and experience oneself is the mind's most powerful tool. On a deeper level, it cannot even be called a tool because it is the essence of the mind. The mind is a highly sophisticated reconstruction machine—it seeks to redefine itself continuously, creating an incessant noise while doing so.

The noise of the mind creates an illusory image of oneself, a false identity, which continuously establishes itself in regard to the surrounding world. This process might appear as heavy judgments or just innocent labeling of any perceived thing, but seemingly everything the mind comes up with is used in reconstructing the false identity, the one which bears the name 'I'. There are no innocent thoughts unless the thoughts arise from a state of inner peace and stillness.

Unlike what people normally encourage, one should not act according to who he or she is. Embracing the patterns of false identity typically leads to destructive behavior. Instead, one should relentlessly try to find out who he or she *really* is, and not settle for the answers which the false identity already incessantly whispers. It would seem the only way to do so is to shed the light of awareness on all the things that one is not—anything perceivable is not the essence of one, not even the mask of identity.

A curious and strong sensation of a hurry, accompanied with a small grain of anxiety, is felt throughout the day. Rationally thinking, there should not be any hurry as everything is getting done on the schedule. Maybe it is only a fear of not meeting the planned tasks in time and all the imagined consequences of such fearful scenarios.

2ᴺᴰ OF FEBRUARY

The pendulum of the false feeling of hurry has swung to an opposite angle. The morning proceeds at its own pace, in its own way. Even though the daughters are late from the daycare and one is dramatically late from work, no sensation of hurry is felt. There is no problem with being late. The problem of hurry arises only when thoughts interfere with reality. Hurry is nothing more than the mind's decision about being in the wrong place at the wrong time.

However, one cannot be in the wrong place or at the wrong time. The anxiety arises only when the mind projects itself in somewhere else than *'here and now'*. When that projection is in conflict with the reality of *'here and now,'* the mind-made identity feels threatened and inclined to fight for its own survival. Lots of unnecessary stress arises. Mind-made stress is a form of psychological suffering which holds no connection to the reality of the world. It is only an illusion which embraces reality.

4TH OF FEBRUARY

The forest is very still and embraced by an intense coldness. The occasional distant cracking of the trees gives meaning to the deep silence of the surrounding nature. It is so cold that all forest life has curled up in itself, and no movement is perceived anywhere. The air is very clean, and the sky is clear. The rays of the morning sun shed a bright light on the white treetops, creating a breathtaking balance of shadows and light. At the moment, the spruce's frost-covered branches are the most glorious sight in existence.

The silence of nature creates an inner space of silence. It is curious how external silence affects the mind; the mind is either rendered silent, or it starts to panic because the false identity the mind has created faces its own illusoriness. In deep external silence, the mind strives to boost the identity by excessive compulsive thinking. Streams of thought easily lead one astray to the imaginary world of time, dispersing into fragments of the past and future.

Today, however, silence is very present.

5TH OF FEBRUARY

Today is cold. Very cold. Not even the wind disturbs the unmoving nature.

6TH OF FEBRUARY

There is absolutely no force or effort in writing this diary, but occasionally a burden is felt by a curious kind of commitment to it. The commitment is experienced only when thinking about the task; there are no exact memories of what the first pages contain, and there is no clue what the remaining pages of the year will contain. Every now and then, a temptation arises to look back at the written words and plan the diary thoroughly, to make sure nothing is repeated too many times.

However, the temptation to look back or plan ahead arises only when thinking about the process of writing. Sometimes the mind grows restless and needs to organize and categorize the contemplations written on these pages. The feeling always stays for a little while, and the fingers do not move while it is present. When the mind withdraws to silence, the words start appearing again.

The mind cannot understand that everything can happen without active thinking. Pure thoughtlessness is outside the boundaries of the mind and the false identity it has created. Thoughtlessness does not mean negligence, carelessness, falling into physical unconsciousness, or otherwise becoming ignorant of the surrounding world. Thoughtlessness means that no thoughts are arising in the form of the mind-made apparatus, which bears the name 'I'. Some thinking might still appear in this state of being, but such thoughts only express gratitude for what is and what the world wants to emerge at a particular situation, and nothing more.

The fingers stop moving on the keyboard. The eyes gaze intensely upon the computer screen. A powerful sensation of thoughtless relief is experienced; there is no commitment to writing any of these pages. The writing happens by itself, and whenever someone reads these words, the reading happens by itself.

Nothing is mandatory in the experience called life. A total renunciation of all commitments creates the value for every commitment one makes.

7TH OF FEBRUARY

The light blue morning sky opens its heart to the souls who are willing to see. No clouds block the vision, and the magnificently bright half-moon painted in the canvas of the sky welcomes the pristine being of anyone gazing its glory and stillness. The soul is in a state of undeniable and uncompromisable peace.

8TH OF FEBRUARY

The hum of the airplane penetrates the consciousness, embracing everything as the whole body resonates with the hull of the plane. The all-encompassing resonation fades away a little when the wings lift the aircraft off the runway. Even though the sensation diminishes, the experience is still all that is. Although its magnitude has changed, it seems to fill everything in the awareness.

As the airplane rises above the curtain of clouds, the horizon expands everywhere, colored with hues of red, orange, yellow, green, and blue. The deep and dark blue sky above dominates the view, but it can only do so because of the beautiful colors of the horizon. Without colors, the magnificent darkness above would have no meaning at all. The night turns into the morning. Occasionally, the city lights can be seen in the darkness below through the holes in the clouds.

Distant lights of another airplane catch the attention. The airplane is barely seen, but still recognizable as an airplane. From their viewpoint, this particular airplane looks just the same—both points of perception observe something tiny in the distance while being something very present 'here'. Both are in the distance and yet 'here' at the same time.

All existence is based on the experience of being *'here and now'*. The experience is the same, regardless of residing in a physical or mental realm. Even in dreams, there is a certain feeling of being *'here and now'*. The all-encompassing experience of *'here and now'* is what everything in existence shares. It connects two points in the opposite reaches of the universe in the same way as it connects two airplanes in relative proximity with each other. Whatever the viewpoint is, it is the center of the experienced universe. Whatever viewpoint one perceives from, it expresses the very essence of all existence.

There is nothing more beautiful than existence.

9TH OF FEBRUARY

Existence is a vast creation. The question is not by whom or what it was created. Any question will lead the questioner profoundly astray whenever the answers are expected from external searching. There is no creation outside of the *'self'*, and even the act of asking a question or awaiting the answer is a creation within the *'self'*. The answer to a question never asked is in plain sight, in every single experience one can be aware of.

One's personal experience is all that is. There is nothing external that can be reached. Additionally, there is nothing internal that can be found. Everything is just what it is, and nothing more. Any thought one thinks, or action one commits, is the creation of oneself.

12TH OF FEBRUARY

The wind blows the snowflakes against the face. It creates a conflicting sensation of simultaneous discomfort and bliss. The mind feels unease because the face feels cold, but at the same time, the body enjoys the cold breeze on the skin. The strong sensation of cold tells the body it is alive. There might be some discomfort in living, but there is an absolute enjoyment in just being alive.

Whenever the mind takes over one's actions, the sense of being alive recedes. The tingling in the fingers and toes disappear, the feeling of warmth in the chest is gone, and breathing is entirely ignored. Everything that remains is the continuous voice of thinking. Thinking is a sign of life in itself, but the symbolic world it creates bears no connection to being alive. The connection to life bestowed by thinking is abstract and creates an entirely different world than the actual reality.

Thinking should not be suppressed, though. Forcing the streams of thought to stop in radical refusal, for example, meditating with an intent to grasp an empty mind, will lead to a more disguised mind-made identity. True meditation is always a state in which there is no mind, and where no mind is present, there cannot be any reaching for results. Before meditation, one should always question why the meditation is exercised. Even the smallest grain of expectation will lead to a state of an empty mind, which is an inherent part of the mind-made identity also known as ego. Only when one realizes that there is no reason at all to meditate does the whole life become a meditative process. Only then does the meditation become the physical state of the emptiness it usually reaches for.

Life is a process of becoming aware of oneself. One can become aware of life only in inner silence. The silence is the unjudging awareness of the discomforts and comforts of the body and the mind. It is not a forced silence, but a silence that will happen purely spontaneously.

Right now, the silence is the cold breeze felt on the face while walking through the light snowfall.

13^(TH) OF FEBRUARY

The younger daughter's temper tantrums have been absent for a while...until this morning. Only when the wife states the fact aloud does one realize the relatively long absence. Noticing the present outburst, and being aware of the few weeks of their absence, a curious peace is felt emanating from the crying child.

The memory of the absence and the reality of the presence of things lift each other up in a mutual arising. There cannot be an experience of something without nothing, and there cannot be an experience of nothing without something. A bird without wings cannot fly, but the wings grant the bird the ability to fly. The freezing cold outside would be an absolute experience—in other words, *all that is*—if there was not the experience of the warmth of the house. Suffering would not feel like suffering if there were no pleasures to remember. The suffering would feel

51

absolute, and in its absoluteness, it would contain a sense of profound peace and inner stillness. The dawn of a new day would not have its meaning if the night were not preceding it. The life that one is aware of is *all that is*. Thus, it creates a state of primordial peace with all its ups and downs.

Inner stillness prevails when facing the daughter's temper tantrum. Giving attention to the curious peace and stillness emanating from the crying child, the child's state of being seems to shift to the same stillness. Apparently, on some level, the daughter senses the same peace. A mutual appreciation and gratitude for the tantrum arises, but also a realization that it does not have to be. The appreciation leads to a stillness that is owned by no one, but that can be sensed only when the mind stops its compulsive behavior for a while. The total silence of the mind creates a space for the stillness to emerge through a multitude of behaviors and forms.

14TH OF FEBRUARY

A profound revolution of the mind takes place while walking toward the office. A paradigm shift in the way of thinking happens very spontaneously, without warning. Total attention is given to perception and objects in awareness. The profound shift occurs without any labeling or judging at all, and it brings about a curious realization.

Nothing will ever be the same again.

Everything seems the same as before, but nothing is the same. With the wings of that realization, in situations throughout the day where the arising of thoughts should normally happen, an absence of thoughts is perceived. The false identity is entirely absent and utterly silent. The absence of the mind-made identity does not affect the appreciation of things; just the comparing, judging, criticizing, and labeling entity within is gone. Objects within sensory perceptions are experienced more clearly than ever before. The death of the false identity is not the end of everything—it is the beginning of life.

Without striving to be or achieve anything, Valentine's Day's flowers are brought to the wife. A profound sense of gratitude and love extends from that small act of appreciation and courtesy.

16TH OF FEBRUARY

Life is a curious kind of a rollercoaster. Procrastination with a certain thing has apparently hurt the wife's feelings. Whatever the hurt is and whatever feelings it might produce, they are only patterns of forms. The feelings in two different human beings are forms that arise mutually, bestowing a sense of reality to one another.

However, if identification with the feelings cease—in other words, one knows that the feelings are only personal, but not essentially oneself—the feelings in another also start to gradually follow the same path of awareness. The feelings depend on each other, and the anger in another cannot live if it does not hear echoes from the other's feelings. The absence of echoes does not mean a lack of compassion—it means journeying deeper into the world of the feelings, observing and perceiving, and before all, deriving the sense of the self from the state of being instead of the feeling.

In all mishaps and catastrophes lingers a compassionate face of existence that is hidden in plain sight. All unfortunate events carry within a seed of fortune. All inconsiderate acts withhold a meaning of love. Love is always there, and one just has to seek it instead of plunging into the illusory world of the false identity. Whatever the false identity creates, is not true because it is essentially a tool for seeing what is not true. Through this, it acts as the vehicle for finding out the truth.

Even though frustrated feelings and thoughts arise for most of today, a strange sensation of peace and stillness is sensed. The inner stillness compassionately and patiently witnesses the frustration. It does not judge the feelings in any way but accepts them totally as they are. And in that acceptance is uncovered a deep sense of love and appreciation for oneself. Through the unconditional self-love, love for the wife and her feelings is regained.

The pendulum of life can oscillate only in different vibrations of love. Nothing else exists but love. However, this love is not the conceptual love described by thoughts, but simply the openness and acceptance of all that is.

20TH OF FEBRUARY

The day is freezing cold. An eerie fog covers the landscape. The sun cannot be seen, but its rays penetrate the opaque wall of whiteness. Everything is very still and peaceful, despite the traffic and continuous background noise in the city.

Anywhere the attention is turned to, restless minds are seen trying to find their own peace in the world. However, the effort to find peace prevents most people from finding it, and if they do find it, it is only a temporary state of achievement. The illusion of peace that can be attained through actions is the reason most humans suffer. True peace lies only in the relinquishment of the false identity.

The mind cannot experience a state of being without the false identity because the mind is identity itself. Thus, any effort to attain a personal transcendence is a form of a most skillfully disguised identity. Nothing the mind does can reach the peace for which it deeply longs. All doing—as well as thinking as a form of doing—creates resistance, and all resistance disappears only when no force is applied.

Seeking, which is the nature of the mind, does not occur in the stillness. There is nothing to seek, and no one seeking. If any force is needed to attain the inner stillness, one reaches only an illusory and temporary state of an empty mind. A mind, which is empty by force, cannot make room for the absence of false identity. It cannot reveal the stillness of being. The existence is unimaginably subtle, and any conceptual contemplation of it breaks the peace with which it occurs.

21ˢᵀ OF FEBRUARY

The nature of all thought is constriction. Identification with thoughts suffocates the joy of being alive.

22ᴺᴰ OF FEBRUARY

A cold and gloomy ambiance embraces the evening. A flock of birds circles above the landscape. Their constantly changing and moving form is barely seen against the darkening sky. The movement of the flock is unimaginably sophisticated, and whenever the birds change direction, it happens with such an immense internal harmony and graciousness that the mind cannot grasp its deepness.

The distant flap of hundreds of wings creates a sensation of a soft wind every time they circle over. Also, the dog seems to notice the graciousness of the moment as it sits very still for the whole time—something it rarely does. The flap of the wings whispers of nature's way of appreciating and loving itself.

26ᵀᴴ OF FEBRUARY

The weather is peculiar and breathtaking. The soft wind lifts up tiny particles of ice and snow from the ground and rooftops. They form small vortices in the street, and as the icy snowflakes swirl in the air, the bright rays of the sun scatter amid their beautiful dance. The whole street is covered with sacred light. The tiny crystals shimmer in the air like they were made of light themselves. Only one thought is whispered silently in the mind:

Light is the primordial form of the creation of existence.

Every moment is creation. There is nothing that is not created in the vast happening of *'here and now'*. The existence does not have a seed from which it grows, and it does not act as a seedbed for accumulation. There has been no past, and there will be no future. There is nothing that was, and there is nothing that will be. Life as an experience is a wave between two infinities, which render life to nothingness. The mind cannot understand it because it dwells in the realms of its own illusion of time—an illusion which takes place only *'here and now'*.

A sense of love resides in the nothingness. It is not a place or a state of being, but literally nothing. It cannot be attained, reached, or grasped because it already is. There is nothing outside, nothing external. All that is, is found within.

The beauty of creation is the crystals of ice dancing in the air and bathing in the embrace of healing light. What is aware of it all? Nothing.

How can one not feel compassion for everyone else when the nature of one's own mind is revealed? The revelation cannot come through teachings, books, gurus, authorities, beliefs, opinions, or anything external. The revelation can come only with the direct experience of what is, most importantly through what the mind is. Self-knowledge is found only in pure experience.

Acquiring self-knowledge through experience does not involve any effort to change oneself. If an attempt to change arises, it is only an act of a conditioned mind, echoes from the past. The essential nature of everything does not seek to change anything. If there is any change sought after, the seeking happens in the unchanging nature of everything.

'All that is' does not seek results. The true nature of the world is not results-oriented and does not care whether the result of a particular happening is good or bad. Anything seemingly good or bad is only a thought, a comparison between the present moment and memories. Everything will end up in the same clearing in the forest. All paths lead to the same mountaintop. Constant seeking for results is only an arduous path for reaching the destination. 'All that is' cares only about every single step that is taken.

28TH OF FEBRUARY

A strange freshness is felt in the air, and the freshness reflects also in the mind. Everything is new. Everything is pristine. The day feels like it is the coldest day of the winter so far. Only a distant chirp of a lonely bird breaks the silence in which the whole perceivable world lies.

MARCH

2ND OF MARCH

Gazing upon the snowfall from the office window. The unusually large snowflakes fall slowly down to the ground. A strange and intense experience of the physical dimensions of the surrounding space unfolds, and yet the experience is aligned with an inner sense of no dimensions.

The greatest miracle in the world is the awareness which can perceive and sense something within itself. There is nothing more miraculous than the subtle experience of being a subject perceiving an object. Those two can happen only in mutual arising. Without one another, the subject and object would both be rendered to nothing. Together, they are an expression of something that gives rise to everything. And the space between creates a sense of separation. Without the space between, the subjects and objects could not be.

Only by experiencing oneself as the awareness— the space between, and that which "gives rise to"—can one realize the miracle of the self. Conceptual knowledge is not enough, as it resides only in the realms of the mind. No thought-based contemplation is needed to unveil the deeper self, and actually, most of the times such contemplation is only the mind's inner resistance in disguise.

There are no tricks or methods to find the deeper self. No external teaching or guru can ever lead one home to oneself. It is not a goal to be reached for, as it cannot be reached at all. Reaching for the revelation of oneself while sitting in meditation might not reveal it in a whole lifetime. A spiritual way of life might never open the doors to the miracle of awareness. One must give up everything one has ever learned, and in doing so, relinquish every single grain of expectation. All that is needed is to have an effortlessly still, yet alert mind while confronting the world. And in the stillness of the mind, one realizes that not even that is required.

In the peaceful and timeless essence of it all, the snowflakes still hover slowly to the ground. Nothing has changed.

All minds hold within something that seeks conflict, that loves to breed hate and anger. One might say that no conflicts are wanted, but they are actively sought nonetheless. The conflicts might appear as an open declaration for war or just a small and seemingly insignificant sign of irritation. The mind cannot be aware of those conflicts because the mind is the conflict itself.

After waking up from the afternoon nap, a strange sensation emerges. It feels overwhelming, yet subtle and untouchable. The view of the forest in the window and the whole perceived world feels inescapable. Nothing else exists at the very moment, but the view of the snow-covered forest. At first, it feels frightening. The simplicity and imminence of the experience creates some panic in the mind, but very quickly the threatening feelings fade away. Only the simplicity of the existence of awareness remains, and it triggers a realization:

'I am' even before the simple perception of the world.

When one is, has been, and always will be before one's own perceptions, then one is truly untouchable. No happening in any life situation will jeopardize the sacredness of one's innermost being. Nothing that happens can ever create a victim of anyone as the essence of everything *is* before any circumstance.

4TH OF MARCH

The fell is a resting place for the soul and mind. It bathes in the bright sunlight, and the landscape far below is a painting of stillness. The forests around the fell are partly covered with thick snow, and the small lakes scattered within the forests seem like white portals to nothingness.

The family needs attention as much as the magnificent view does. In perfect harmony, the image of the beauty of nature is left behind, and undivided attention is turned toward the children. Any effort in trying to grasp even the most beautiful thing in the world will beget suffering when the world needs attention elsewhere.

Much of the beauty that is usually experienced are thoughts. The stillness of the landscape has a gravity that attracts the mind to accumulate thoughts around it. The view is labeled with different adjectives describing beauty. Impulses arise to tell others about the same experience. The mind races on to create thoughts of contentment. However, thoughts can at best only describe the thoughts of contentment—the mind is a closed circle.

As one realizes that the real contentment lies beyond thinking, one also realizes that all the beauty of the world is held within. The beauty of the landscape has practically nothing to do with the landscape. The entire awareness is turned toward the noise of the children, and the same beauty and utter importance are still experienced.

The thinking mind cannot know real beauty, but only abstractions of it. "I feel at peace" as a thought is only a superficial pointer to the peace experienced within. Pure experience of inner peace cannot be categorized as peaceful because it just *is*. Pure experience involves no time, which would create the possibility of labeling the experience.

5ᵀᴴ OF MARCH

The morning sunlight covers the fell with its golden rays. No clouds obstruct the view to the majestic dominator of the landscape. The eyes rest on the powerful contrast of the clear blue sky behind the fell's silhouette. No strain of thinking or the burden of the conceptual identity is present. The weight of the snow pulls the branches of the trees toward the ground, creating a visual image of a forest of snow-white pillars, reaching toward the open sky above.

It's intriguing how life operates through gravity. Gravity can exist only when two or more objects are gravitating toward each other. Without the objects, it could not be. Gravity also creates inherent resistance within the objects, observable as a pushing force, instead of the externally perceived pull. Life uses this resistance to fuel its growth. Without resistance, the entire existence would have already happened.

The mind is an apparatus of resistance. It redefines the false identity through resisting the circumstances and conditions of the surrounding world. Whenever resistance arises, one is close to a greater truth than what the false identity can ever offer. Whenever a lack of openness and acceptance is perceived in one's own behavior, the stillness within operates on the level of perception. Resistance might arise in realizing the stillness within, and the false identity might struggle and fight for its survival. In letting all resistance be, without changing it in any way, the resistance will subside and reveal something deeper than the mind could ever have imagined. As all resistance fades away, the essence of everything becomes obvious.

6TH OF MARCH

The freezing cold air embraces the white forest. Everything bathes in the brightness of the day. The snowflakes glimmer in the sunlight like diamonds, filled with beauty beyond words, dancing in between the snow-covered pine trees. The slow falling of the snowflakes on the blanket of pure white snow creates a sensation of something timeless.

The new snow covering the ground this morning is very peculiar. A handful of the snow feels lighter than air. All the individual snowflake forms can be seen perfectly. The little snowflakes are embraced by a lint-like frozen substance—icy crystals that are too small to be perceived with eyes. All snowflakes share the same foundations of existence, but none of them are the same.

All forms are passing, and in every death resides a joy of creation. The snowflakes melt and turn into water on the bare palm. The breath blows the remaining light snow easily off the palm, and the whiteness scatters in the air, slowly falling down to the ground. Afterward, an intense feeling of presence emerges, lasting most of the day.

9TH OF MARCH

Compulsive thinking is a state of a mental cramp. If the streams of thought continue, the mind eventually goes into a "muscle cramp," curling up in a mental fetal position. However, nothing can be done to stop the streams of thought but to be present. And to be entirely and utterly present, one must not do anything. Stopping the behavior of compulsive thinking is not a doing, but the ceasing of all doing.

When all doing ceases, the stillness of one's own true nature is revealed. It does not necessarily happen instantaneously, but it will happen over time. If an expectation of it occurs, it is only the compulsive mind at work.

While lingering in the stillness and the emptiness of the mind, some thoughts will most likely appear. Some feelings may arise also. Even opinions and judgments might surface. That is when they can be truly observed, and their illusory nature is revealed. Their actual nature is not illusory because they are an intrinsic part of ultimate reality, but deriving one's identity from those thoughts, feelings, opinions, and judgments, and perceiving the world through them is an illusion.

When thoughts and feelings are perceived without judgments, a new sense of identity starts to emerge—one that is not based on egoistic desires and does not thrive on conflicts. This new sense of identity appreciates and is grateful for every experience the reality bestows upon the self. The more it surfaces, the more oneness is felt with the rest of the world. The more it stays, the more powerful it will be when interacting with the multitude of circumstances in the world.

Every sentient being has the opportunity to realize the unity they share with the rest of the world. That's when the thoughts lose their overwhelming power over simple reality. Experience of oneness awaits to be revealed in every single moment, and ultimately at the end of every road. And ultimately, one may realize that no road is better than another. Despite their differences, they all lead back home.

10TH OF MARCH

The inner stillness is not the same as the silence of the thinking mind. It is not something that can be directly achieved by silencing the mind, but through the silence, it can be revealed. When the mind is compassionately rendered silent, one can feel something new and fresh underneath. Something that has always been there. The silence of the mind creates an opening, where one can experience oneself. This experience is not created as a memory in time, but it is a pure experience that does not need time to exist.

If a pure desire and an intention for a deeper inquiry about life arises, all one has to do is to watch the openings. Nothing else is needed.

11TH OF MARCH

The daughters are playing cat and mouse. Despite the distinct contrast and tension between the roles, they play as if the cat and mouse were friends with each other. They perfectly convey the behavior and gestures of the animals, fully submerging into their roles in the play. And the roles are pre-decided. They do not fall into the unconsciousness of opinions or animalistic instincts but rise above such things. Even though being animals to their fullest understanding, they remain friendly with each other. No suffering of any kind is involved.

Communicating with children is curious. It is a play of identities, where one might refer to oneself as the "dad," and the child calls herself by her own name. There is no such ego investment involved—that is usually known as the "me," which prevails in most adult communication. Often, interacting with children easily slips into the egoistic establishment of the identity of the "dad" and the child— into parenting. But on a very basic level, communicating with children withholds no two serious identities that could establish any kind of an authority problem.

Life is a play in which different roles are adopted. What is usually called "me" is one of the most changing patterns one can ever know. Thinking of "me" as something constant creates a seed of suffering because "me" and everything regarding "me" is nothing but constant. However, every single moment in life also holds within it a way of being free of suffering. Such a way will be found with full certainty if close and undivided attention is given to the world unfolding at the present moment. Being free of suffering is the essence of all life.

12TH OF MARCH

Every encounter with another human being is sacred. In all encounters there is an option to choose who and what one decides to be in comparison to another human being. Despite the sufferings or pleasures brought by another, one always regains the possibility to choose either love or fear, acceptance or rejection, openness or closing. It is all just a matter of perception and perspective. Grief, anger, hatred, sadness, or any other negative feeling does not mean one has to impose negativity on another through actions or thoughts.

Projecting one's own negative thoughts into another human being is utter unconsciousness. All thoughts and feelings happen within oneself—another has nothing to do with them. Only in total unconsciousness, one might hold another responsible for one's own life situation. The unconsciousness in human relationships is the dwelling place for the ego, and only the ego can suffer.

The portal out of suffering is true selfishness. Not the egoistic selfishness that seeks to be something in comparison to others. The most selfish thing one can do in this world is to let others be just as they are, without striving to change or judge them in any way. Only such selfishness can lead to unconditional loving of oneself, and through that, loving everyone else.

The morning is full of light. A multitude of birds is singing their appraisal to the awakening spring. The subtle scent of something undefined in the crisp air feels beautiful, and it offers a clear opening into the presence of the ever-renewing moment of *now*.

13TH OF MARCH

Only the individual experience of oneself exists. It is surrounded and pervaded by eternal emptiness, from which all existence springs. And the being of existence is the foundation for all life. There is nothing outside of one's own being. Every single grain of thought and emotion happens within it.

At first, it feels very lonely during the times when operating from beyond the mind—from the level of being. A powerful resistance arises because the truth felt in simple being is so utterly in conflict with everything the mind has ever learned through its limited perspective of separation. All perspectives of separation include inherent resistance. When this resistance is observed, a new sense of self begins to emerge from beyond the mind. One realizes to be something totally different from the thinking and resisting mind. The loneliness of just being turns quickly into solitude.

In the solitude, when the mind's resistance is allowed to be there without trying to change it, one realizes the nature of oneself: the freedom, harmony, and serenity, which spring from nothing. Everything in existence sings the silent songs of those attributes. One's entire experience breathes through them because without them, the experience of life would not be.

There is nothing else other than this. No thing else.

14TH OF MARCH

The feeling of presence is mostly continuous today. At times it is more subtle, and occasionally it feels more all-encompassing. No effort or force is needed to achieve the state of presence. The presence lingers there in the background of everything. Quietly and peacefully. Practically nothing is done to feel the soothing presence and inner peace.

Today, while staying more or less in the stillness of the present moment, all the routine actions become very slow and peaceful. Impeccable and undivided attention is given to every action committed. Even the most meaningless activities have gained a profound meaning. Pouring the tea into the cup. Putting the shoes on. Writing notes on the paper. Opening the door. Each step in the empty office corridor. Inputting the debit card number in the grocery store. Turning the faucet on. Brushing the teeth. Changing the vehicle's gear while driving. The mind tries to argue at times, how many important things there are to think about, but the impulse fades away as quickly as it appears.

Occasionally, some involuntary thoughts arise, but their arising is perceived before they gain strength to lure awareness into their endless streams. Today, many thoughts are needed to interact with the surrounding world, but none of them seem automatic or conditioned. They do not arise from the typical reactive state of mind. Today, thoughts arise as an action from beyond and before any reaction.

15TH OF MARCH

While browsing through a multitude of books in the office, a strange book is found that opposes everything the mind has learned about the world. Surprisingly, the mind does not launch the familiar conditioned mechanism of labeling the book and the author wrong. All that arises is, "This is not for me now. My state of existence is not served by this, at this very moment."

However, the mind understands that it might change due to happenings or conditions that are unknown at this moment. Someday, that particular piece of information—that strange book—could be the most significant thing in their life. Therefore, nothing should ever be judged as wrong. Labeling anything as wrong leads only to a spiritual and mental diminishment of oneself.

Even labeling something as different is a constricting prison made by thought.

All forms of labeling and judging close unseen doors to the liberation the human mind deeply craves for. The mind goes around in circles until the liberation is attained.

16TH OF MARCH

There is no suffering. Only identification with what appears as suffering exists.

19TH OF MARCH

Intense headache colors everything this morning. The muscles in the neck and shoulders are stiff, and the ache throbs in the back of the head, intensifying and relenting in turns. The pain comes and goes like waves hitting the shoreline. The constant noise made by the daughters and all today's tasks instructed by the wife do not make the situation any easier to handle. The mind stays quiet, though, and only a few thoughts of resistance arise. Despite the headache and the unfathomable amount of information produced by female communication, the inner stillness is felt. Just barely, but it is sensed nonetheless.

When a moment is honored just as it is, everything is embraced by a silent and soothing blanket of inner stillness. A genuine acceptance and appreciation have a healing effect on any situation. Any resistance—in other words, thoughts about what should not be—will create suffering. Aligning with the flux called life, and everything it holds within will erase suffering and have a healing effect on life. Acceptance leads to healing, and as a state of being, it is enough. External circumstances will eventually shift to make manifest the state of acceptance in one's life situation. The healing occurs only '*here and now,*' and its expressions will happen in time.

The headache stays, and the mind advises to take painkillers because there are many important tasks to do today. The mind chooses to believe in the promises the painkillers bear. However, the mind is partly identified as a spiritual seeker, and it scolds itself for believing itself, but the thought floats by very quickly in the spotlight of pure awareness. The muscle stiffness in the upper back lingers for the whole day, but the ache relents soon after taking the medicine.

20TH OF MARCH

Some minor headache and muscle stiffness are still felt today, but painkillers are no longer needed. Like many times nowadays, sitting in front of the computer with this text open in the display, but nothing arises. However, it does not create a single grain of suffering. Writing this is not a necessity of any kind. While sitting in the stillness of the moment, with the display's pale light coloring the face in the darkness of the room, a deep revelation arises.

Nothing must ever be done.

There is nothing that must be done, and nothing exists that would judge the undoing or procrastination in any way. Nothing bears the meanings that one's mind has learned to attach to everything. Anything compulsory is only an illusion, and the nature of all illusions is their non-existence. A compulsion to do something bears no meanings or purpose within. The compulsion exists only in the present moment in the form of a thought or a feeling. All one has to do is to see the compulsion as it arises, and not follow the illusion it creates.

The realization that nothing must ever be done creates a fresh possibility for anything and everything to be done.

21ST OF MARCH

The airplane wobbles as it flies through the blizzard. It dives up into the clouds, and everything is covered in total whiteness. No visual perception is experienced that would create a feeling of movement. Only a slight trembling of the hull of the airplane is felt.

Suddenly the whiteness subsides, revealing a clear blue sky. The immense brightness of the sky almost hurts the eyes. At the same moment, the mind stops completely, revealing the familiar stillness and the aliveness of the present moment. The mind had been raging all morning about myriads of things, without catching a breath, but in the instantaneous and total change of the perceived environment, the mind is rendered silent. The silence lasts for most of today, even though the work in the destination needs much attention.

22ND OF MARCH

A strange vibrating sensation in the chest is felt most of the night. Some intense tingling is also observed in the hands and legs. The heartbeats are sensed very clearly, but none of it seems unpleasant. The cause for the sensations is unknown, and the mind whispers about a multitude of problems the body might suffer. Despite the noise of the mind, a deep peacefulness is experienced in background.

23RD OF MARCH

Nothing exists in the world that one knows less about than oneself. Over time, the mind has learned the ability of thinking in terms of everything else than oneself, and as a habit, the mind sometimes feels challenging to overcome. Ultimately, it does not even need to be overcome, but only observed in total awareness.

A whole dimension of uninvestigated existence lingers behind the mind-made thinking entity. When one thinks of oneself without any conceptual reference point, there is not much left to think about. When thinking ceases, being starts to emerge. In the state of being, many minor details in the surroundings are perceived, that have been obscured by the clouds of thinking.

The world is full of forms, colors, smells, sounds, sensations, feelings, emotions, and thoughts. A certain touch of life flows through every single detail of perception. It has always been so, but only in the silence of the mind, those details can really be observed as they are. Embraced by the inner stillness, one comes to know oneself more in detail than ever, and through details, liberation is realized.

The perception of details is everything needed to live a life of fulfillment and joy. Correspondingly, compulsive and uncontrolled thinking is everything needed to live a life of anxiety and suffering. Unconscious and hidden knowledge in the ceaseless accumulation process of the mind is the root of compulsive thinking. Only will scrutinizing oneself in the space of total awareness loosen those roots.

24ᵀᴴ OF MARCH

The sun shines with a warm embrace, yet it is freezing cold outside. While basking in the rays of the sun, an ambivalent sensation of simultaneous warmth and coldness is felt. The sensations are present with one another, without applying any force to make the other one disappear. Only an occasionally arising thought of coldness or warmth makes the opposite sensation temporarily subside.

The disguise mechanisms of the mind are revealed by tuning into a state of being, that is in conflict with the current circumstance. All one needs to do is to find a feeling of happiness in a situation of unhappiness, and the mind whispers: "That is wrong! You are not supposed to feel happy." Additionally, when seeking a feeling of unhappiness in a state of happiness, the mind whispers: "There is no reason to feel unhappy! You should be happy now!"

When feeling ill, one can create a feeling of not being ill, and the mind says: "But you are ill, you cannot change what is." In a sense, the mind is correct, but one can always change the perspective in which one looks at things. In the face of sadness, there can be joy instead of suffering. Serenity can be manifested instead of anxiety, happiness instead of grief, anticipation instead of regret, or fulfillment instead of lack. External circumstances always withhold the meanings one gives to them.

However, an inner conflict will arise if one seeks to change the state of mind. The mind will not let it happen. Instead, all conflicts will evaporate if the nature of the false identity is revealed, and it is revealed whenever one acts consciously contradictory to what the mind thinks about the circumstance.

25TH OF MARCH

What would be more of a miracle than two perspectives of the same totality gazing into each other's eyes, embraced by eternal, unlimited, and timeless nothingness? The all-encompassing embrace of infinity renders any given moment to nothingness, from which the miracle of existence springs.

26TH OF MARCH

The strange sensations in the chest keep on surfacing more than before, especially during moments when the mind lets go of its endless tasks and to-do lists. Almost immediately, when all active doing ceases, the feeling is there. The strange vibrating sensation has turned into an unpleasant feeling of fullness in the chest, accompanied by a slightly painful experience of heartburn.

Some unjudging and compassionate awareness is present with the body's discomfort, but the mind wanders easily into thoughts of more dramatic causes of the condition. Whenever the mind stops, the discomfort turns to pure physical discomfort, and in the plain and simple experience of it, the acceptance of the experience starts to blossom. The mind is capable of only adding mental discomfort to the situation, making it more challenging to handle.

The mind has a curious habit of making itself restless. If one is identified with the makings of the mind, one becomes the restlessness.

27TH OF MARCH

Today consists of much human interaction. It is easy to get lost in the different levels of relationships. Getting lost means being unconscious of one's own habitual thinking, and the unawareness of the present moment. In the unconsciousness, selfish motives are not seen. In total awareness, the ulterior selfish motive of every single action becomes clear.

Everything can be traced to its origin—the experience of the self. Every thought, word, and action is selfish, and nothing else. One cannot commit anything that would not be selfish. The mental position of selflessness is the most unconscious selfish belief one can ever adopt. However, as one becomes aware of the selfish motives behind everything, true selflessness starts to emerge.

The road to true virtue and pristine selflessness always goes through one's innermost self. The realization of the self is continuously in plain sight. One only needs to look directly at it, without the veil of thinking, without giving time to oneself.

The heartburn and a sense of pressure remain in the chest today, reflecting much uneasiness to the relationships during the day.

29TH OF MARCH

The heartburn and a lump in the throat absorb much attention. Normal activities in life seem to have faded away. Only a few times today, a feeling of connection is felt to the surrounding world, to the beautiful wife, and to the playing daughters.

The body is physically present all the time, but thoughts have created a totally different reality. The continuous streams of thought feel relentless, but no resistance arises. Natural flowing with the streams occurs, without regret nor scolding oneself of not achieving the inner peace. It feels curiously soothing to feel present feelings and to drift in the streams of thought.

The mind ponders on what might be causing the physical condition, and some fear arises with physical pain. Fear of the unknown. It is very curious how the false sense of identity strengthens in pain and suffering.

APRIL

1ˢᵀ OF APRIL

The emergency room bed feels soft and a bit cold. The clock on the wall ticks loudly as every second move to meet the next one. The air is cool, and the nurse has laid a warm blanket on the bare chest and abdomen. Some anxiety is sensed in the body and mind, but the relentless ticks of the clock leave no space for anxiety to fully arise. The ticking of the clock acts as an anchor to the presence and inner peace.

Many tests are taken while spending quite a long time in the room. In the middle of it all, the room suddenly looks very different. Everything is more vibrantly colored and shaped. Significantly fewer thoughts run through the mind. The room seems to be more full of light, and necessity arises to check if the sun shines through the window. However, it does not shine at all at the moment. The light seems to be everywhere, embracing everything from the outside, and emerging from the inside of all perceived objects.

The light is subtle. Whenever occasional thoughts flow by, it disappears, leaving behind dull white walls and a dim fluorescent lamp hanging from the ceiling. The interaction with the nurse and the doctor steals the light temporarily. When left alone for a while, the light fills up the room again, and thoughts cease to arise.

Everything is profoundly well, despite lying in the hospital's bed with the wires of electrocardiography device and blood pressure monitor attached to shoulders and chest. Nothing could be more perfect than that. Whatever happens, happens with inexorable perfection.

2ND OF APRIL

The river rests silently under a blanket of ice and snow, and the whiteness of the snow glows beautifully in the bright sunlight. It was not long ago that the river flowed free under the same sun, and it will not take long until it does so again. The river flows when it flows, and that is all it ever needs.

The heartburn is still felt in the chest, but the sense of identity is not derived from it at the moment. The same physical feeling that produced anxiety and mental suffering before has turned into peaceful awaiting. The mind has decided that in time, the river will run free again.

The false sense of identity is deeply rooted in every single thought. Whenever a thought arises, the object of the thought is already a thing of the past, and in the same way, any identity rooted in thought is a reflection from the past. Thoughts are images of something, that occurs in the present moment as a memory. No true identity can be derived from them—they produce only illusory images of the past.

The same goes for all physical sensations. The wind on one's face has already happened, when the mind creates a concept of the "wind on one's face." The brightness of the sun in one's eyes is only a memory when it is perceived. A question lingers in the back of the skull:

What remains if a sense of identity is not based on thoughts?

Nothing is left, and in this boundless clarity, one can feel how all forms spring from the primordial emptiness. The emptiness is never replaced by forms, yet sometimes one gets lost in those forms if they are mistaken as replacements for the emptiness. Ultimately, pristine stillness remains, and it cannot be touched or altered in any way by the forms arising in it. In that all-encompassing stillness, the entire world is utterly without protection, and perfectly safe.

In the embrace of timeless eternity, the river will run free again, and again, and again…

3RD OF APRIL

Small, light snowflakes fall down from the sky again. Nature procrastinates the coming of spring, as if it was something that must be done, but is put off a day after another. However, a curious perfection is seen in all procrastination, if the results-oriented mind is rendered silent.

Efficiency and procrastination are both beautiful perspectives of creation. The creation will happen whether or not procrastination occurs, and being in inner peace with procrastination sheds beauty to all things that are not getting done. Creation does not judge anything as done or not done. Pure creation lies in the stillness of the mind and the peacefulness of the soul.

5TH OF APRIL

The air is humid and still. Birds sing their appraisal to the morning and the coming spring. Their songs are full of anticipation and joy, and the distant sound of the motorway creates a soothing rhythm in the background. Only an hour of sleep was gotten during the night, and the sleep deprivation affects the ability to focus.

When taking the daughters to the daycare, the mind seems to occasionally drift away into streams of passive thinking, where no clear thoughts arise. Some abstract out-of-the-context thoughts sometimes appear, lasting only a fraction of a second. A few times the mind is caught in a state of an empty stare. The mind shakes off from the passive mental state by trying to pay more attention to the surrounding world.

The mind is everything that it is and should not be anything else. If there is any reaching to become something different, the mind plays tricks with itself. It reconstructs the false sense of identity through inner conflicts; the mind decides what it should not be, even though it is just and only that. The false identity does not want to be tired when it is tired, angry when it is angry, or shy when it is shy. The mind builds the false identity on expectations and requirements, which create the foundations for external situations to produce inner conflicts. Inner conflicts always carry suffering within.

Whenever enough awareness of one's own thoughts is present, the illusion of the false identity and its conflict-filled reconstruction process become more transparent. Eventually, all illusions evaporate into thin air. The awareness must be non-intrusive and not interfering at all. If any interference is exercised, the mind plays tricks against itself once again. Liberation cannot be found in the kingdom of the mind.

6TH OF APRIL

The temperature is well above zero. All the ice and snow are melting, and deep slush covers the roads. Really focused attention must be given to where each step lands, to avoid getting the shoes wet. Just before reaching the car, a tiny stream of water on the ground catches the entire attention.

The small flow of water—just a few centimeters wide—winds in between the tiny slush mountains. It is perceived as small, but it flows with a habitus of a great river, making its way through the vast icy mountain range like it has done for millions of years already. The silent elegance of the river entirely engulfs the awareness. The feet stand still. The eyes gaze intensely. Thoughts stop happening.

Timeless perfection resides in everything perceived, no matter how great or small, meaningful or meaningless the thing is. The same vastness and elegance can be found in the smallest possible details like in the whole universe. Nothing is more insignificant than something else, and nothing is more significant than anything insignificant.

8TH OF APRIL

An intense sensation of choking, lasting a few seconds, forces an awakening in the middle of the night. It is a clear symptom of the severe phase of acid reflux the body is going through. The heart beats wildly. The mind rages on about death and all the possible consequences of death, and how it would affect all the loved ones. The mouth is parched, and a big lump is felt in the throat. The mind relives the sensation of choking over and over again, producing the fear of death over and over again, as if it was trying to make the thought of dying the most important thing at the moment.

The mind always seeks to resist death, but it can only do so through thoughts concerning death. This is how it creates lots of unnecessary and redundant anxiety around the concept of death, and around quite much everything negative in general; repetitive thinking of something that is unwanted grants that something a reality.

There is nothing wrong with the fear of death. It is a by-product of the evolution of the human mind. Fear is a natural emotion. However, continuous and incessant thinking of what is unwanted creates much suffering. The mind is a mechanism which seems to be tuned to think about unwanted things because of the need for survival. Thinking about unwanted things makes them important in a very peculiar and counter-intuitive way. Even though one thinks the unwanted things are not important, and uneasiness arises while thinking of them, the mind still needs to make them important by thinking of them.

No thought should be given to anything unwanted. If a thought concerning something unwanted arises, one should think again of another perspective on the matter at hand. Then think again. And again, and again, until the behavior of the thinking mind and its tendency to conditioned and unconscious thinking is revealed. In this revelation, the inner stillness unfolds. The mind stops. Everything is just the same, yet nothing is the same anymore. Things have no meanings. Thoughts have no meanings.

Sitting a few hours in the bed before laying to sleep again. The mouth is parched and a big lump is still felt in the throat. The night is magical in its silence.

9TH OF APRIL

The sky is wide open. No clouds are drawn on the light blue canvas of the sky. Gravel crunches under the feet as while walking. Walking happens without any particular means to an end. It is just walking, one step at a time. The air is warm. Inhaling feels pleasant, and exhaling relieves the body of all tensions. Breathing happens without any particular means to an end. It is just breathing—inhaling and exhaling in a natural rhythm. The sun shines brightly, dominating the vast sky. The greenness of the pine trees creates a distinct contrast with the blue sky. The birds sing loudly in a tree nearby. A few bikers go by, then a car, and afterward everything is quiet again.

Silence emerges. Silence, which has always been there in the background, like the clear sky above. It is so obvious, yet so subtle that no attention is given to it in the realm of the mind.

10TH OF APRIL

Early in the morning, a ragged lady approaches in the street. The same lady has approached a few times in the past days and she's always in need of a small amount of money. More often than not, people walk by her without giving any attention. Mostly they look away in resentment and do not make any effort in communicating with the ragged lady. Sometimes they just raise their hands as if they were busy doing something else, without even glimpsing her.

As she approaches, the body stops and a smile appears on the face. The more rooted one is in inner stillness, the more acceptance and unconditional compassion one feels toward other sentient beings. This compassion is, in fact, compassion for oneself that one sees in another.

The lady's smile is beautiful, and her eyes are friendly. Only by stopping the unconscious routine of walking to work, can her face be seen as it is seen now. She asks for money, but no money is carried at the moment. That particular communication pattern is only an empty function of the two identities—no money is even needed. Only a few words are changed, and that is sufficient for both beings.

Everything done in a state of pure presence is always sufficient. There is no lack of anything in presence.

13ᵀᴴ OF APRIL

Two birds play in the air silently and elegantly. Their complex dance is an image of perfection. Their movement is so fluent and spontaneous that it stops the mind completely. As the mind stops, the sun is seen as it shines from behind the treetops. Its rays penetrate the crisp air, creating a faint contrast of shadows and light on the ground. An airplane moves in the distance. It leaves a wake of steam in its path through the open sky. The airplane and its wake slowly fade into the vast openness of the sky. The sky is utterly peaceful.

Whatever is experienced peaceful, is a projection of the inner peacefulness. Objects, conditions, and situations do not carry peacefulness within. They do not and cannot hold the sentient concept of peacefulness. All peace one experiences is an expression of the inner state of stillness. The peaceful sky is the peace within. The peaceful lake is the peace within. The peaceful forest is the peace within. The presence of a peaceful person is the peace within.

As long as peace is sought from external objects, persons, or situations, the peace will remain time-bound, and therefore temporary. There can be no peace in the past or future. The peace can only arise 'here and now' if the arising is allowed. Allowing it means total acceptance of all that is.

No peace would exist if one did not exist. All existence is primordially a product of inner stillness and even calling it the inner stillness is only a concept.

14TH OF APRIL

Ice and snow are melting at a tremendous speed. Every day the ground seems different, as the piles of snow diminish. The sun is relentless during the days. The melting layers of ice reveal tarmac roads and small areas of dark and muddy remnants of grass. The grass seems dead, but a subtle aliveness is sensed in the black ground. Some other plants have also appeared from below the surface of the snow, still waiting for the perfect time to start growing and blossoming. Every time is perfect for the plant life to flourish, and if it does not happen at all for whatever reason, it is perfection in the purest form. The cycle of nature is impeccable in its perfection.

The rebirth of nature happens again soon, as it has done over and over again. It reminds one of mortality. Whenever one becomes aware of one's own mortality, the illusion of immortality fades away, and every single thing becomes important and special in a sacred way. The joy of just being alive arises—even though life occasionally means pain and suffering—and no time is left to think redundant and negative thoughts. Being face to face with the experience of mortality does not leave space for judgments, opinions, destructive mental positions, compulsive and conditioned behavior, criticizing, comparing, or even fear. Any fear regarding mortality is only a belief, an accumulation in time.

The illusion of immortality arises when one identifies with the mind-made and conceptual 'I', that seeks its own continuity and survival. The false identity believes, that to survive, there must not be any thoughts concerning mortality, and if there are, they must be seasoned with fear. Mortality means the limitations of the thinking mind, and whatever is unknown to the mind is automatically approached with some aspect of fear. The mind blindly seeks its survival through the knowledge it has accumulated in the past. In the stillness of the mind, mortality is seen as the perfection of existence. The embrace of mortality allows life to breathe freely, without fear, and filled with unconditional love.

Every living being in existence ceaselessly approaches home. In the eternity of all that is, the journey through time is rendered to nothingness. Perceiving life in everything and everyone means already being home. That experience reveals inexorable and immovable stillness within.

17TH OF APRIL

The more aware one becomes, the more clear are the moments when one gets lost in thoughts. The awareness cannot shine through during the streams of thought, but afterward, one inevitably awakens from the slumber of thinking. The contrast becomes more and more distinct when awareness is more frequently present. The process of awakening might be slow and take years, or it might be instantaneous.

The awakening does not bring salvation because any salvation is a product of the mind—a conceptual idea of finally arriving somewhere. Awakening is not arrival to salvation. It only implies ever-moving continuance and immovable stillness. Words and concepts can describe it on a very shallow level at best.

There is nothing that can be done to make the awakening process faster. Any action taken regarding awakening or enlightenment is a creation of the mind-made identity, which has purely egoistic and self-important drivers. Awakening is not a result of some particular deed or virtuous life. Enlightenment does not come through accumulated knowledge, nor through the seeking of enlightenment, which is a consequence of accumulating knowledge.

Life includes openings, through which the light of awareness shines. Whenever the light of awareness is sensed, one realizes there is nothing else than it. The realization of *nothing else* brings forth peace, calm, and tranquility.

18TH OF APRIL

The airplane rises elegantly, accompanied by a loud noise of the turbines and the resonance of the hull. Fierce wobbling is sensed as the wind pushes the airplane sideways, resulting in some anxiety. Starting a week apart from the family, and already some longing for home is felt. Occasional thoughts appear, whispering that something might happen during the flight or the travel in general, that could threaten one's survival. The mind creates stories about how the wife and the daughters might cope after that. The fear-induced stories then turn to the feelings of longing once again.

In the mental state called normal, the mind lives in a constant feeling of lack. If no observable lack is present, the mind tends to create an imagined lack, projecting it quite often in the future in the form of a vision of losing something precious. However, the true nature of everything is perfection. Even the most painful state of lack is perfect in its innermost nature.

Losing anything—either actually losing or just imagining it—is a piece in the perfect mosaic of life. This piece has an underlying purpose written into the fabric of every single experience:

The one having the experience is life itself.

There can be no comfort in the state of lack if the perspective is the mind. There is an all-encompassing comfort and peace in all pain and suffering when the perspective is life. In the realms of time, the pain and suffering might never go away, but absolute comfort is found in the timeless. No fear can exist in the state of pure being.

19TH OF APRIL

The outcome of a situation is always the sum of the situation and the perception of it. Whenever the perception is changed, the outcome grows to be different. The ultimate outcome is always the accumulation of every step taken on the path. It depends on whether the perception of each step is propelled by sincere openness or a closed and limited image of oneself.

20TH OF APRIL

Awakening, which is also called self-realization, does not involve anything spiritual. No belief-based physical or mental exercise can be executed to realize the self. Self-realization cannot be attained because it already is. It cannot be revealed because it has never been hidden. It cannot be gained because it has never been lost. It cannot be grasped because it has never been released. More so, it cannot end or die because it has never been born.

Whenever the self-realization comes, it occurs as an opening in the fabric of consciousness, the very root of one's identity. It occurs as an indescribable feeling of opening the eyes even though they have not been closed or awakening without having gone to sleep. It is a total paradigm shift in one's state of being—a one-hundred-and-eighty-degree-turn from the outside world of identity and compulsive thinking to the inside world of stillness. In that stillness, the roots of identity are realized and embraced by a soothing emptiness.

21ST OF APRIL

It seems that if wild animals are given food, they develop a tendency to return to the feeding place over and over again. Their presence becomes more frequent the more food is served. Thoughts are like animals when they are given attention. They become more frequent, and they start to stick to the one that is feeding them. Eventually, the feeder begins feeling and believing the thoughts as a part of oneself. As a part of the identity, the thoughts always manifest in the surrounding world in one way or another.

No belief is ever carried without a counterpart in physical reality. Thus, physical reality always acts as a mirror reflecting one's own thoughts and beliefs.

22ND OF APRIL

The sense of 'I am' creates an opening unlike any other. As the root of identity, it draws concepts to its heart like a magnet. Its gravitational force is irresistible. 'I am' is the primordial concept and the cause of the sense of separation. But when 'I am' is given full and undivided attention, everything dissolves, including the sense of 'I am'.

23RD OF APRIL

The medieval fortress whispers quiet words of ancient times. The ravens sing their harsh song somewhere in the distance. The stone walls are very still. In the middle of the crowd of tourists in the courtyard, an enormous tree rises up to the heavens. It is ancient, and the stillness it radiates is breathtaking. However, very few people seem to even notice the tree. They are enchanted by the history of the place, their minds filled with conceptual knowledge.

The mind contains a curious habit of seeking protection inside the knowledge it has accumulated. It feels threatened by things that are known to be harmful. And everything unknown is always possibly harmful from the perspective of the mind. It has built walls around its knowledge like ancient people have built walls around their fortresses. The mind tries to defend itself against anything that might prove its accumulated knowledge wrong.

Mental defense positions lead to seemingly right-minded deeds. Righteousness is the path to destruction. Non-judgmental compassion and acts of giving exercised with an open mind are the basis of all abundance. An open mind is the propellant of pure creation, an afterburner of unconditional love.

Walls and trenches can never create abundance. All they create is limitations, and limitations lead to frustration and fear. Abundance is created in being open and true to the surrounding world while reaching for the open skies above like an ancient tree in a crowded courtyard.

26TH OF APRIL

Water pours down from the heavens. It is still cold, and the gusts of wind shake the leafless branches of the trees. The forms of the trees tremble and change with the wind. The shift in their forms is perceived as a strange and unpredictable wave-like motion. Despite the weather, a multitude of birds sings their songs to the awakening nature. Their constant chirping and tweeting are hypnotic. Every single sound they make is profoundly different.

What seems as repetition is never a repetition. Nothing in existence happens *again*. Every moment of the eternal now is unlike any other moment. The subtle ongoing process of creation depends on the destruction of what has been created, and whatever is destroyed can never exist again as the same. The perception of existence shifts in every possible moment of creation so that nothing can ever be described as happening again. The ongoing wave of destruction and creation is beautiful. Deep peace is connected to it.

The daughters are now in the day-care. Sitting in the car, listening to the chirping of the birds of spring and watching how the raindrops explode and disperse into millions of tiny drops of water when hitting the car's windscreen. Some thoughts concerning everyday routines arise occasionally, but a delicate sense of peace and stillness are present. The stillness usually unfolds when no thoughts obstruct the perception. But sometimes it unfolds during thinking as well. In such moments, it manifests as compassion toward one's own thoughts.

27ᵀᴴ OF APRIL

The realization dawns as inevitably as the sun rises from beyond the horizon:

All my life, I have been scared of myself.

102

Being scared of oneself is the foundation of a false identity. The powerful realization stops the stream of thought that has extended over the whole morning. A soothing stillness and experience of deep presence arise.

28TH OF APRIL

The crisp morning coldness in the air emphasizes the long shadows of the trees. The forest is a beautiful portrait of shadows and light, and the silence is broken only by some distant chirping of birds. The snow, trees, and ground create a rich mixture of white, green, and brown. When thinking occurs, the colors collapse into concepts and thoughts, that abstractly model the colors. In the gaps between thoughts, the mental appearances fade away, and the colors of nature seem very authentic and alive.

A secret lingers behind all appearances. All forms are fueled by it, but most of the times thinking obstructs the revelation of that secret; thinking creates appearance and if all that one sees is thoughts, the connection to one's own individual secret becomes lost. However, it cannot be truly lost because one can never be disconnected from it—only a temporary state of oblivion can occur. Nothing worse than that can ever happen.

The most unnoticeable emotions are the clearest pointers to that secret. If emotions are denied, one denies oneself. Even the most subtle emotion screams for attention. It craves to deliver the message of the very meaning of one's own being. To find one's purest meaning, the deepest emotions need to be found, without compulsive thinking obstructing the way, and then lead life appreciating and heeding this continuous flux of emotions. The flux can be only '*here and now*', outside of the illusion of time.

29ᵀᴴ OF APRIL

Water slowly drips to the ground as the snow melts on the roof. Some birds dance in the air between the pine trees, and a soft scent of the forest is sensed as the damp ground is partly revealed from below the melting layer of snow. The trees giving shelter for the birds' dance are very still, yet moving in slow and very subtle rhythms.

Everything is moving at different paces. The birds flying in the sky, the cars driving in the motorway, the people walking in the street, the trees rising up to the heavens. Even the most seemingly immovable object is moving and changing constantly. However, when all movement is observed from a point within—the stillness that lingers beyond all appearances—the movement is rendered to nothing. No movement can ever occur, as the ultimate reference point is an eternity. Eternity, which cannot have an opposite, which is the immovable presence of everything that contains only what appears to be moving, yet is essentially still.

30TH OF APRIL

The fell's silhouette in the distance against the light blue sky seems vividly alive, as the morning sun lights the white snowy surface of the giant. The soft wind brings sensations of ancient and timeless being, which rests upon the forests of life. The aliveness is everywhere one looks. It is so evident, and in plain sight, that one loses the experience of it time after time. Any effort in grasping the experience pushes one away from it. The ceasing of all effort reveals it.

MAY

2ᴺᴰ OF MAY

Taking the daughters to day-care early in the morning. They do not co-operate very well, which leads to silently growing irritation and anger. The mind starts to create stories about being late from work, and it requires the children to behave as is seen right from the mind's point of view—the only right there can be. Everything else is plain wrong. However, children have a tendency to do everything else, which fuels the mind's irritation. Not even the shortest break in the streams of thought occurs.

Afterward, when walking back toward the car, the familiar stillness arises out of nowhere. It embraces everything. No thoughts are present. Just a peaceful silence within. There are no memories of the morning's negative emotions and no expectations of getting to work on time. When swaying in the warm embrace of the inner peace, a sudden spark of fear is observed. The fear feels very primordial.

Coming into contact with nothingness feels scary. An urge to back away from nothingness arises as if it was a burning flame scorching the life out of the body—a matter of survival. But nothingness is not the end. It is merely a state of being where the identity has evaporated. It is the essence underlying every single characteristic of the identity. The false identity fears nothingness because its survival is dependent on the ever-continuing habit of compulsive thinking. When compulsive thinking stops, the false identity perishes. With its last breath, which can be quite a long one sometimes, the fear of the unknown arises.

All fear is a product of love. Love is all there is. Not the conceptual and clinging type of love, but an unlimited and unconditionally compassionate love, which accepts *everything*. Nothing is left outside of it—this love is all that is. At some point in all human lives, fear starts to creep in, and the mind always falls in love with the fear.

Every single action is propelled by love. Love fuels the positive things in life as well as all the negative. Nothing is ever experienced without being open to it on some level, without loving that particular experience. Even the most destructive emotions are fueled by love. Accepting *everything* will lead to a world filled with unconditional love, an unlimited openness that remains in the eternal moment of *now*. One does not need to change in any way to realize it.

One does not need to become anything to see the truth. Only stillness and letting go of the false image of oneself is needed, and this does not require any effort or force. When all doing ceases, resistance also ceases, and the world shifts into loving reality.

3ᴿᴰ OF MAY

It is miraculous and mind boggling how one always arrives at a place and time called *'here and now'*. Sometimes the awareness of it is lost, but the awareness is always regained over time. A moment in time incessantly changes into an entirely different moment, and in the crossroads of every single moment the *'here and now'* arises. It always does, and it's always the same unchanging experience. No matter how long a journey it has been from the last realized present moment, the present moment always feels the same. Only vague and selected memories remain from the gone present moments, which define the experience inside the moment. But memories can never define the moment itself, much like letters can never define the blank space of the paper on which they are written.

All things and situations will eventually pass. They will rise and fall like the words in this book. As the pages are turned one after another, the past pages are no longer experienced but only as a memory. The future pages cannot be experienced but only as an expectation. Only the word that is perceived at the moment is all that matters. *'Here and now'* is the only thing that can hold reality in place—it is the foundation for all existence. All else is illusory, just dust in the wind.

Everything is temporary. Realizing the ephemeral nature of reality anchors one firmly in the present moment.

4TH OF MAY

A strong urge for salvation burns deep within the human soul. It can be seen in the eyes of a random passerby in the street and felt in another human being in temporary relationships during the normal business day. The urge for salvation can be sensed in the heart of close, intimate, and permanent relationships. The will to be saved seems to dictate most actions people commit in their daily lives, even the most routine and insignificant ones. The longing for the survival of the image of oneself suffocates and strangles the mind, which itself is the architect of this longing.

The bleak form within that seeks the survival of oneself is not the essence of humanity, but a curious and mechanical part of the mind that unconsciously creates an illusion of being an identity. The urge for survival, which produces much suffering, is a mechanism that protects the illusory false identity while being an integrated part of that identity. However, the false identity cannot be saved. There is no salvation it can ever achieve. It can only strive for salvation, creating much bliss or havoc on the journey to the destination, but the false identity can never reach it. Permanent salvation does not exist. As the urge for survival and the seeking of salvation cease, reality unveils as it has done an infinite number of times before.

While spending most of the workday in the peaceful state of being and natural alertness, numerous situations are observed when the unconscious and automatic survival instincts arise in other people, and in oneself too. One is not different from the others in any way. The same mechanisms are at work inside every single identity. The survival mechanism can be seen in routine and minor interactions between two or more people, as well as in the more significant happenings during the day. Everyone seems to think they have something to protect. Apparently, everyone feels they need to accomplish or become something for being protected. The vivid aliveness of such a hidden thought is clearly seen only in full awareness.

Life is not a battle that can be won or lost. Salvation, if there is any at all in the sense of the concept, is to realize the true nature of the self. Life is a process of saving oneself from the oblivion of non-realization. The process cannot *not* be done, as eventually every single particle of consciousness will rise up from the sea of unconsciousness, and bask in the glorious yet subtle and humble stillness of its own essence.

Thinking can never bring salvation but can offer only a temporary bandage on the bleeding wound. One must go deeper into the very nature of thinking and the thinker, to realize the essence.

Much comfort is found in observing that a few times during the day at work, there are openings in the stream of individual and collective thinking. During those openings, the light of consciousness shines through, healing everyone present. Not many seem to notice it, as they go back to the realms of their minds to rant and rage about other problematic things. But those who notice it, seem to keep it with them the rest of the day, even without knowing what it is.

On some level, writing this very text is a huge pitfall. Whenever pure awareness recedes, and the symbolic intellectual contemplation is all that is left, the pitfall will engulf the consciousness. Only the unveiling of pure awareness is salvation, and no words are needed for it.

5TH OF MAY

Driving back home from a long day of celebration and meeting up with relatives. The daughters are sound asleep in the backseat, and the wife is about to doze off. The last rays of the sun shine brightly in the rearview mirror, and the light colors the treetops with astoundingly beautiful orange color.

The mind and body are tired, even though the whole day was quite pleasant. Just a few moments away from the destination, two majestic swans appear, crossing the skyline. Their elegance is breathtaking. The pure whiteness of their feathers makes them seem like two distant suns in the sky. Immediately, the familiar stillness uncovers from beyond the thinking mind. Inner peace is projected without any kind of a filter to those magnificent creatures dominating the bright evening sky. Their presence is unwavering. The presence is sensed in each flap of the wing, that leads the beautiful white beings from an unknown journey to an unknown destination.

The pristine feeling of beingness emerges from underneath all perceived reality, leaving only what is, and nothing else. Nothing unreal remains.

6TH OF MAY

Seawater seeps through the melting layer of ice as the sun sheds warmth on the awakening nature. The sea looks like a vast living organism, with a multitude of faces and veins of water wandering on its skin. The surface of the ice glows like a thousand newborn suns. A cold and light breeze blows from above the melting icy vastness, and it brings up spiritual thoughts.

No matter how spiritual one's thoughts are, they cannot present the reality but only on a shallow and illusory level, which has very little or nothing to do with reality itself. Whatever one thinks is, is not. Thoughts are mere abstractions and illusions covering the ultimate reality. Realizing and experiencing this does not necessarily change the ultimate reality in any way, but the perception of it changes. As the perception changes, it means the perceiver, the one who has the experience, has already changed.

The younger daughter and wife are vomiting in a relentless embrace of stomach flu. Some subtle stress is felt about it. The mind whispers how much better life would be if everyone were healthy right now. However, despite the stress, no resistance at all is sensed toward the situation. Acceptance is total today. The melting of the sea ice acts as an anchor to inner stillness, and at the same time, the slowly changing sea is an external expression of the inner stillness. When directly experiencing the ultimate reality, there is nothing that can be defined as inner or outer. Everything is part of the same immensely sophisticated and beautiful symphony of eternal waves.

7TH OF MAY

People seem restless. On some level, the surrounding restlessness deepens the awareness of it all. On another level, it affects the mind, producing restless streams of thought. The whole day is a pendulum between conscious presence and unconsciousness.

The mind seeks to fill itself up with external stuff. Whenever a void occurs within the patterns of thought—a lack of some routine activity, a profound change in a life situation, or even a lack of thoughts—the mind puts much effort in finding something to fill the void with. In other words, the false identity called the 'I', is constantly striving to become something. It can do so only by seeking external things, which it can then claim as its own.

When the hallucination called the 'I' is noticed, it disappears. Only presence remains when the false identity evaporates. In presence, a curious observation is made:

The 'I' that one thinks themselves to be is included only in thoughts concerning the 'I'.

When no thoughts about the 'I' are present, identity does not exist. The false identity, which most people believe to be, is only a pattern of thoughts that arises when there are thoughts present. Without thoughts, identity is not.

8TH OF MAY

The mind is an interesting piece of machinery; it will not stop, and its most shining creation—the identity—thrives on resistance. The more one resists the makings of the mind, the more powerful the illusions grow.

10TH OF MAY

The sea is still mostly covered in ice, but the solid white surface recedes quickly day after day. A huge wide opening has formed in front of the shore, and the water is very still in it. No waves whatsoever can be seen on the surface. It is a mirror reflecting the sky above, resting in harmony with surrounding nature.

Standing on a massive rock on the beach. The rock still radiates the deep coldness of winter although the sun shines with friendly warmth. The rock has been there on the beach as long as memory goes, but it is never the same. Today, the rock is not a rock, but an expression of the inner stillness, and the spaciousness of a profoundly silent mind. The coldness of the rock creeps into the body through the bare feet, but no discomfort is felt. Only hints of neutral physical sensations are observed, rising and falling like waves in the ocean of awareness.

Two birds fly across the still water. They dare not touch the surface, as if they were honoring the silence the dark waters hold within. Their brilliant and unique airborne dance reflects perfectly on the surface of the water, and it seems if there were four birds instead of just two. The birds move and dance, and there seems to be no end to it.

The silence is deep today. The soul is very still.

11ᵀᴴ OF MAY

The daughters play and jump on the trampoline. Their carefree joy lights up the beautiful day even more. The dog lies in the shadows, hiding from the warmth of the relentless sun. Occasionally, the dog flinches as a bee flies nearby. The air is almost still. Only one windmill is lazily rotating far across the bay. The absence of wind makes the day even hotter, and a strange conflicting sensation arises with the vision of the sea. It is still mostly covered in ice, yet the warmth of the air feels like midsummer.

Nature is magnificent in all its phenomena, which create a multitude of experiences within oneself. Everything in nature screams silently to be noticed without any interpretation or labeling. The whole surrounding world constantly points to the very being of one's own nature.

12TH OF MAY

Nothing similar exists. Every single grain of existence feels different—the rocks on the beach, the trees in the forest, the people paddling in the slowly opening sea, the birds singing, the soft and damp smell of the forest ground, the small areas still covered in ice on the beach, the gentle heartbeats within the chest. Everything emits a strange radiance of variety and difference. Everything is unique. Life will never be the same again.

Two birds swim in the sea. They occasionally disappear as they dive under the surface, only to appear some distance away. It is impossible to tell where they will rise to the surface again, and they usually spend quite a while diving. Every time the birds appear, great delight is felt within. The joy is similar to a small child's feelings during repetitive plays. To the child, there is no repetition, but only joy.

13TH OF MAY

The tree stands tall and motionless against the sky, as it has done innumerable times before. A few clouds roll slowly by in the background. There is no haste whatsoever. Despite the light wind, the tree's leafless branches stay motionless. The branches are like veins in the human body, first diverging from the trunk of the tree into dominant and massive branches, and then one by one scattering into ever smaller versions of themselves, spreading out in all directions. The self-induced spreading of the tree creates a vivid impression of life that can be sensed only in the stillness of the mind. The tree stays silent and motionless against the blue sky. The soul stays silent and motionless with the sky and the tree.

14TH OF MAY

Back in the city. The trees have started to blossom. Small green leaves have appeared to color the skeleton-like branches. It feels like whole nature is suddenly exploding into different shades of green, and a subtle scent of grass is occasionally sensed. Traffic is relentless. All the background noises make the mind a bit restless. Profoundly different kind of thoughts arise in the vicinity of civilization than in nature. An entirely different identity lives within while taking care of the routine stuff in the incessant hum of the city.

The identity one bears within is highly ephemeral. It is the most changing thing in one's life. It changes as fast as situations and conditions change. The identity changes because the thoughts connected to situations and conditions change, and there is no identity but the one found inside every single thought. All thoughts have an intrinsic part of identity in them. In the absence of thoughts, identity does not exist.

Thoughts are not illusions, but thoughts create illusions. Everything unreal disappears when one opens the unjudging eye of awareness. In the world of the mind, many things block the arising of true and ultimate reality. So many unreal things. When one identifies with thoughts, *being* has been mistaken for an illusion of *becoming*.

What is left when there is no identity involved in consciousness? Words cannot answer the question. Only being, and patient waiting in stillness can. However, there can be no expectations for the answer. Only in the void of all expectations, the answer unfolds.

15TH OF MAY

Today, the mind seems to judge the tendency to become present. The natural alertness, which arises in the present moment, is not a natural state for the false identity because it thrives on concepts of the past and future. The mind seeks its meaning, and the very purpose of its existence, through labeling and conceptualizing, which can happen only in unison with the idea of time.

As the natural awareness of the present moment arises, the mind creates thoughts of importance. It whispers: "There are so many things in your life more important than this moment... This moment does not bear anything meaningful within... You cannot become anything by focusing on this moment only... You are nothing unless you do this or that... You should be focusing on doing rather than being still within... You are wrong..." All the continuous whispering brings forth a smile.

The mind is eager to grasp the state of nothingness and turn it into a concept because the identity cannot exist in the nothingness. The whispering is only a set of protective maneuvers—the silent urge for survival in the most hidden corners of the mind. As more presence and alertness unfolds, a realization arises that silences the mind completely:

There is nothing more important than the present moment, whatever it holds within.

16TH OF MAY

What is first a game of joy, will become a burden after one identifies with the game. Life, when taken too seriously, becomes chained in the weariness of the world. When the childlike behavior and innocent view of the world disappears, so too disappears the unconditional joy. There is always a multitude of things in the world to regret and worry about, to be concerned about, to grieve about, to fear, and to think about. However, the game of life is fundamentally not about such things.

The game of life is not about attaining something, then losing something, and once again gaining something. It is not about searching and holding on to the precious things the mind values. The game of life is best played when one flows through life with no resistance. The absence of all resistance creates unconditional joy and happiness, which are the foundations for all existence.

17ᵀᴴ OF MAY

The morning sun feels warm. A cool breeze caresses the skin. Traffic is relentless, as usual, but it does not create unease. Every direction the eyes look, an inner peace emanates. People seem somehow happy, more open to one another. While walking down the street toward the office, many people lift their heads up and look straight into the eyes, smiling. For some reason, this morning makes people shrug off the virtual reality of thinking, and connect with each other. Not on a verbal or conceptual level, but on the level of being. Sincere smile always arises from the level of being.

21ˢᵀ OF MAY

The footsteps echo loudly in the empty stairway. While searching for the office keys in the backpack, a thought appears out of nowhere. It is the same thought that has risen every morning for a few weeks already, without exception. "I should mark the office key in some way because the backyard gate's key looks very similar. They get mixed up many times in the keychain." The thought remains for a while. After unlocking and opening the office door, it disappears, and other thoughts come pouring in. A subtle smile appears on the face while observing the streams of thought.

All thoughts seem to be similar to those thoughts concerning the keys. They are triggered by something in the current environment, only to be replaced by other thoughts when the environment changes. Thoughts are not independent and separate occurrences inside the mind but connected seamlessly to the surrounding world. They arise when certain events arise. They disappear when the events flow by, and when something else arises. Different environments trigger different kinds of thoughts, based on what knowledge the mind holds within.

The identity created by the mind is nothing different. It is one of the countless ephemeral things the mind creates. Different aspects of identity are triggered by different situations. When they arise, the experience feels unique and personal but is, in fact, a result of something happening outside the boundaries of the identity. The identity held within the mind is deeply rooted in the surrounding world and is subject to the whims of the world. Such identity reflects happiness if the world bestows happiness, and it reflects unhappiness if the world bestows unhappiness. The identity everyone bears within is only a pattern of thoughts connected to the events in the current environment.

The fallacious mind-made identity is only a vague reflection of the self within. In the silence of the mind, the false identity is revealed, and even though it might not disappear anywhere, one realizes how unnecessarily seriously one has treated it. The false identity is nothing serious. It is only a clutter of thoughts. As the realization of the nature of identity arises, the smile deepens on the face.

22ND OF MAY

Life is a meditation. One has only dived so deep into it, that the very foundations of life are forgotten. They are searched for everywhere but from life itself.

23RD OF MAY

It is strange, yet painfully simple, how the experience of *here and now* always occurs in the same way. It has nothing to do with external objects. It happens only in inner stillness. The experience of *here and now* cannot be found in perceivable objects, and it does not bear any signs of its existence. Any external object that exists in the present moment is only an expression of the *here and now* and through their expressed forms, objects connect to the very essence of the present moment.

24TH OF MAY

A small bird lands silently on the grass of the backyard, near the hedgerow. It is some distance away and noticed only from the corner of the eye. No attention is given to it at first. However, the bird stays immovable and gazes adamantly and curiously the human being's actions on the terrace. The attention gravitates toward the little creature's resolute gaze. As soon as the bird gets the undivided attention it was clearly waiting for, it starts moving.

The bird takes a few jumps toward the terrace and then stops to gaze. Again a few jumps, and gazing. Little by little, it approaches. The bird holds an earthworm tight in its mouth. A few jumps again and the bird is so close that the hand could almost reach and touch it. More gazing.

A deep unity is experienced in the situation. There is no bird gazing and no human being answering to its gaze, but only a totality remains where the gazing happens. '*Here*' and '*there*' have lost their meanings completely, and only the space between remains.

The immovable situation must have lasted for several minutes. Then spontaneously, the bird starts jumping away, with the worm still in its mouth. The bird's smooth and elegant movements take it further away, and then the human being returns back to the chores on the terrace. A warm and peaceful sensation is felt throughout the body for the rest of the day.

26TH OF MAY

Much irritation is present this evening. Agitated words come pouring in through the mind. Anxiety breathes heavily within. A hurricane of thoughts swirl in the mind, engulfing the whole consciousness. Total identification with thoughts prevails.

Occasionally, an automatic learned movement of the mind occurs and seeks the stillness within. The mind is desperate to attain the state of deep peace experienced so many times before, but it is unable to do that. In agitation, the mind tries all kinds of techniques to get rid of the anger and irritation. All the trying only worsens the situation. The movement of the mind points toward the inner world, so the external world observes the behavior probably as calm as ever, but there is a storm inside.

Any effort in becoming still is a movement. Pure and sincere stillness does not demand any kind of an effort. If any force is exercised to find the peace and stillness within, the mind only plays tricks and illusions about peace and stillness. It can emulate the silence within in incomprehensibly vivid ways.

After noticing the effort to become still, all efforts cease. Immediately, the familiar and pristine stillness arises within. It is very subtle at first. The hurricane of thoughts still swirls inside, but it does not feel so serious anymore. It does not engulf the entire consciousness as it did just a moment ago. Slowly, but inevitably, the inner stillness grows stronger. Silent gaps appear in the streams of thought. The anxiety is felt stronger in the body than in the thoughts, and in the body, the feeling is more neutral. The body does not hold so much aggression as the mind does.

The focus of attention centers on the feeling of the body, and suddenly, all thinking stops. The feeling in the body is warm and tingling and bears no signs of the anxiety anymore. The inner peace blossoms. It also seems to affect others as the situation starts to diminish into an ordinary course of life. Such is life—a rollercoaster of thoughts and emotions, all of it preceded by the stillness within.

JUNE

4TH OF JUNE

The sounds of the wind blowing through the leaves of the aspen tree act as a vehicle for awakening. Many days have gone by, busy with the workings of the mind, concerned with all kinds of external things. Only memories of the inner stillness remained. Some futile attempts to reach stillness have only deepened the identification with the mind and thoughts. All efforts to reach inner peace have produced much psychological strain. All efforts to relax have created only tension.

Now, suddenly in the middle of a whole day long stream of thoughts, the flickering of the aspen's leaves and the cool wind on the skin create a cessation of all thinking. It feels like waking up from a dream, into an entirely different world. All things are still as they were, but their presence is sensed: the aspen tree, the grass, the sky, the wind, the sand, the rocks, the people, the dog, the house, the car, and the background noise of the motorway close by. An appreciation for everything, even the inanimate nature, arises from deep within. The appreciation has always been there, only obscured by the makings of the mind.

As the aspen tree sways in the wind, a sense of unity drifts into awareness. The gentle swaying of the tree is all that remains. This unity is not any kind of hypnotic meditation, but a full acknowledgment of the tree—total alertness of all the movements of the tree. With the alertness, something is felt that has been forgotten, something that has been overlooked for many past days of compulsive thinking—the *self*.

The presence of oneself embraces everything in a familiar way like many times before. The mind tries to move toward it, but the self cannot be grasped or embraced in any conceptual way. Appreciation and gratitude prevail for the rest of the day.

5ᵀᴴ OF JUNE

The morning is still early, and the house is silent. Everyone is asleep, but one has woken up feeling refreshed, long before the dawn of the day. All is still. Even the wind has ceased totally. Immovable trees stand rigidly in the backyard, and no signs of animals are seen. The sky is clear, and its deep blue color slowly grows brighter. A faint scent of grass flows in the cool air, and some occasional sounds of distant cars are heard.

Something magical is always found in early mornings. It is as if nature awakens to an entirely new existence, like a newborn baby. Everything is fresh, and in silence, the awakening is happening. However, it does not happen in external things, but it happens within oneself. It is not a movement of happening, but a change without any change.

6TH OF JUNE

The wind is intense today. Some force must be used to walk forwards. The trees bend in the wind almost violently, and the wild movement of the leaves creates an impression of a surface of a stormy ocean. Waves of wind go through the leaves, and the sound of it penetrates everything, suppressing the sounds of traffic and people almost to nothingness. The focus of attention remains in the wind for a long time.

The wind cannot be seen, but its consequences are easily observable in the things it affects—much like thoughts. Whatever is essential, is many times invisible to the eyes. The behavior of people toward each other is only an expression of the thoughts and beliefs they harbor within. The body could not live without the bacteria invisible to the eye. The birds could not fly unless there was air under their wings. Nothing would exist unless there was empty space in which to exist.

In the stillness of the mind, the inner spaciousness can be experienced. This spaciousness is one of the observable faces of the deeper self. Yet, beyond that, there is more and more space, as space is infinite and eternal. The self within is the basis of sentient human existence, in the same way as a seed is a basis for a tree to grow. The seed is nothing like the tree, but it already holds the tree within. The self is nothing, yet it holds everything.

7ᵀᴴ OF JUNE

The sea is full of foamy cresting waves. The wind rages with a power of the rising summer. The trees bend with the wind, and small drops of water are carried to bare skin from the surface of the sea. A strong feeling of purpose is felt while gazing at the raging sea. True purpose needs nothing more than being to exist.

8ᵀᴴ OF JUNE

The storm has settled during the night, and the sea is covered in ripples and small waves. The sky is like a painting. Water pours down from the clouds on the distant horizon, and the edges of the clouds are colored with a bright golden light of the sun. Otherwise, the cloudy sky contains hues of deep gray and dark blue. The entire nature seems relaxed after the storm winds of the past day. The light breeze caressing the face feels like an exhale of relief.

The exhaling of nature whispers wordless words of an infinite mosaic of existence. Storms exist only because stillness exists, and together, they form a beautiful picture of what is. A sound perfection can be seen in all storms when the mind is still. The perfection does not erase any pain or agony created by those storms but appreciates them just as they are. Whenever negative feelings are truly seen without any resistance at all, they cannot produce psychological suffering but remain as they are until they dissolve into the stillness following the storm.

The ripples on the surface of the sea are like aftershocks of an earthquake. During the rest of the day, the sea grows more and more still, and in the evening, it is like a vast mirror, reflecting the open sky and the occasional clouds passing by.

9TH OF JUNE

Tall shadows of the trees cover the green field of grass. The dancing shadows and light create a strange feeling of transparency. The shadows are there, but only as visual perception. They do not exist as forms at all. All shadows are only the absence of light, and all light gains its form only through shadows. The transparent nature of light makes all shadows just as transparent, and the transparency of it all produces similar experience in one's own being.

Illusions are real only from the viewpoints of other illusions. Thoughts can only delude other thoughts, and beliefs can only lead other beliefs astray. The false identity within the mind is not a tangible form, but just a projection of consciousness—a shadow of existence. Such form is mistaken for a reality when there is not enough light present. Most thoughts are just the absence of presence, the absence of the *self*.

10ᵀᴴ OF JUNE

The energy and intensity in children's play is immeasurable. No thoughts whatsoever restrict their fluent dance of actions and reactions, and the children move and change the play like a flock of birds changes direction in flight. It happens effortlessly, quickly, and in perfect coherence with the rest of the flock. Their happiness and laughter are genuine, entirely without egoistic investments. The whole play is an embodiment of the '*here and now*'.

The present moment can never be experienced through the mind, but only through letting go of all the labels and conceptions of the mind. '*Here and now*' does not hold within any memories or expectations. The presence is felt when the mind relaxes, just like a palm appears when the fist opens—the palm has always been there inside, only unseen because of the fist.

The presence of the children's play draws awareness in like a vacuum. No thoughts remain.

12TH OF JUNE

Despite being late from work this morning, a profound inner stillness is experienced. The streets seem abnormally empty. Only a few souls here and there pass by while walking towards the office. The sun shines kindly, and the sky is partly cloudy.

Occasionally, the mind plunges deep into the patterns of conditioning, repeating thoughts and stories of yesterdays, and planning the days of tomorrows. However, such streams of thought last but a few seconds, until the light of awareness shines through them. It is not a happening of force, but an occurrence of subtle beauty. Whenever the thoughts are noticed, the automatic and compulsive process of thinking ceases. Nothing else needs to be done to attain the inner peace, and even to say it is attained at all is a misconception. The inner peace *is*, and everything else is but fragments of a mirror laid on the peace.

Always, when thoughts disappear, the world seems quite dull at first. The mind despises its own silence, creating a boring and dull view of the world. However, the silence of the mind creates an opening to discover the inner stillness. When one lingers enough in the silence of the mind and the dull world it produces, aliveness of the environment starts to gradually grow. Suddenly, the presence of a tree feels more vivid, the shadows on the ground create a sharp contrast with the light, and the sounds of the birds feel unique and precious in a totally different way—a deeper way.

13ᵀᴴ OF JUNE

Sitting in the sauna at the swimming hall. The heat is perfect, and the atmosphere is peaceful in every possible way. After everyone else has left and the sauna is empty, the older daughter exclaims: "One more minute." One more minute it is, as there is no hurry anywhere. However, those three small words leave only one clear idea as an echo in the air:

Time is the present experience of memory or expectation.

One can always and only experience the present moment, in which there is no time involved. One minute can never be experienced but only in memory or expectation. The experience occurs in the flux of being, flowing through the so-called minute one step at a time. However, that one step is all that is. No steps exist before the present moment, and no steps will come after it. Any memory or expectation occurring in that moment is based on conditioning, leading to a variety of different experiences in different vantage points of life.

Even a small fraction of time like one minute is experienced in entirely different ways. The child's one minute bears profoundly different meanings than the adult's one minute. An adult's one minute is completely different from another adult's one minute, as numerous factors contribute to the experience of time; the situation, the mental position of the mind, and the energy level of the body.

Sometimes one minute flies by surreptitiously, and at other times it feels like an eternity. In either case, the still presence is there during every step of the way—the only step there can be.

14TH OF JUNE

Immediately after waking up, a powerful sense of presence emerges, accompanied by a strange feeling of a primordial memory of the same presence. Even though one has been absent while sleeping, the self has been present even there. It is something within that does not sleep, has never been born, and can never die. It has always been present and awake.

The memory of presence after waking up is a weird feeling of having been there during the night, but having no memories whatsoever of it. The transparency of it all makes the feeling weird, but contemplating it a bit further, there is nothing weird in it. One's whole life is full of presence, of which there are no memories at all. The entire identity is only a set of filtered and selected memories, creating a sense of self full of stories and causes and effects—the surface self in the chaotic world of external things.

The *self* beyond the surface self is something much more. It is not a product of external things, but all external is a product of it. It is not something that has been born in this world, but the world is born of it. It is the silence from which everything emerges, and into where everything eventually falls and dissolves. The *self* is the stillness of the deepest sleep, yet eternally fully awake.

16ᵀᴴ OF JUNE

The narrow road goes a long way through the forest without making the smallest turn. In the distance, it tightly turns, disappearing behind the trees. A sudden feeling of emptiness emerges as the awareness follows the road into the silent sanctity of the trees. The identity harbored in the mind disappears with the road, and only awareness remains, attached to nothing.

A curious sensation of separation and unity are felt at the same time. Their mutual arising creates a strange feeling of simultaneously existing in the mind and outside the mind. The worlds of attachment and non-attachment exist at the same time, and for a fraction of a second, the perfection of it all is seen. The perfection is always there in the background, though it cannot be seen in the world of attachment, which is in other words the kingdom of the mind.

The perfection of existence is simple, and one experiences it mostly through non-attachment. Non-attachment does not mean disregard, but the experience of reality as it is. This reality includes thoughts and everything that can be observed without plunging into the dream of thinking. Only when observing and committing actions without any thought filtering the observations and actions can the deep meaning of non-attachment be realized.

Counter-intuitively, the state of non-attachment brings one closer to external things. At first, it appears as total separation from external things, but through the portal of non-attachment, the unity of all things is revealed. It is not conceptual knowledge or experience, but something deeper, which gives rise to all knowledge and all experience.

17TH OF JUNE

The mind is a labyrinth of unnecessary information. It is full of illusory corridors of identity. Any effort in getting out of the labyrinth will only deepen the corridors. Any effort in changing the labyrinth will only change the internal alignment of the corridors. After all efforts, the complicated nature of the labyrinth still remains.

Immersed in the labyrinth of the mind, one feels that the world cannot be trusted. If the world cannot be trusted, ultimately oneself cannot be trusted. Without trust for oneself, dark times will inevitably arise. Only through trusting the world and oneself, can the darkest times pass away. It is simple, but not easy. The hardest part of it all is to remain simple. The labyrinth cannot offer such simplicity.

The false identity is a vicious cycle, leading itself to destructive patterns only to find out that those patterns devour the trust in oneself and the world. There cannot be liberation without full trust in everything that arises in the sea of consciousness. That sea is a picture of perfection, as all the pleasures and sufferings negate each other in it, leaving behind only the stillness that existed before it all.

18TH OF JUNE

Lying in bed in the evening before going to sleep. The sun still shines, painting the treetops with bright hues of green. Some dark clouds gather in the distance, and heavy rain falls down toward the land on the horizon. The family is away for a couple of nights. The silence of the house emphasizes the inner silence within. The occasional chirping of birds sanctify the silence every time it is broken.

The sense of just being is not interrupted in any way. No thoughts whatsoever are attached to the experience of it, and when thoughts arise, they are immediately seen. As they are seen, they fall just as quickly as they appeared. From nothingness, into nothingness. The intense sense of being sanctifies every seemingly external aspect of life, leaving only life itself as it is.

No problems are present in the mind nor the body. Despite the body going through flu, and all the coughing and sniffling, the presence stays immovable. It is untouched by the conditions. When untouched, the malfunctions in the body or the mind do not act as problems but are just constantly changing patterns of forms. There are no problems in change. The presence of the moment continually merges with one's renewing perception of reality, and everything becomes one.

After lingering a while in the soothing stillness of the *self* within, sleep comes. The memory-driven mind shuts down completely. The presence remains, without any imprints of memory.

20TH OF JUNE

One does not need to change at all to realize the stillness within. The problem of the mind is that it strives for permanency and certainty, but it can never allow stillness or anything unchanging. The mind does not know how to *not* change anything. It is desperately attached to results, instead of the intrinsic peace of the process.

21ST OF JUNE

In the middle of the night, a severe headache paints the whole world with its discomforting colors. The slightly prolonged flu and all the coughing deepens the physical discomfort. The back of the head is pounding in rhythm with the heartbeats. Existence in the body feels cruel.

The night is deep, yet the sun shines through the curtains. The silent breathing of the family fills up the air. No sounds whatsoever are heard from outside. Nature is asleep. The external silence points distinctly to the body, as it has become tense while carrying the headache. Instantly, when the awareness flows into the body, all the muscles relax, and breathing becomes deeper. Not in the way of an intended meditation, but expressing a natural state of relaxation and flow of breathing.

The headache remains, but all thoughts concerning it disappear with the relaxation of the body. The bright sunlight draws a few precise lines on the wall, creating shadows that embrace the light. Something profoundly mystical is felt in the sunshine in the middle of the night. A car drives by, and then everything is silent again. Inner stillness continues to unfold despite the headache. After some time, the sleep comes back again.

22ND OF JUNE

Cool raindrops fall on the head and shoulders. A distant rumble of a thunderstorm occasionally flows in the air. Everything is very still. The trees are totally immovable. Not a sign of a moving leaf can be observed, and nature is intensely silent. It is almost midnight, yet the world is full of sunlight, scattering through the thick layer of clouds.

The midnight sun brings about a sensation of the light of consciousness. That light is eternally shining, and nothing exists that could dampen its presence. Shadows can be cast by some things within the light, but the shadows are only expressions of the light. The light is always there, and it can be seen only through reflections and shadows.

142

The balance of it all is undeniable. Love embraces all aspects of that balance.

The usual spiritual contemplation ends suddenly, creating an opening for the light of consciousness to shine through. The mind is rendered still. The last remains of the contemplation hover in the air like the anticipation of lightning, accompanied by the raindrops falling from the sky.

Thinking creates rain. In the stillness of the mind, it rains, but one does not get wet. The rain does not affect oneself even though the knowledge of rain occurs.

23RD OF JUNE

The sound of the waves hitting the shore is deep, full of subtle continuous noise and occasional, more powerful rumble. The sounds of the sea merge with the whispers of the wind blowing through the forest, and together they create an all-encompassing totality, expressing the mystical beauty of existence itself. All other sounds of nature seem to integrate seamlessly into the dialogue of the water and wind. Even the noisy play of children is an intrinsic part of it all.

Nothing is wrong. A profound harmony is felt within and without. Internal and external experiences melt into each other and in the embrace of that impenetrable presence, all effort ceases, and nothing else remains.

24ᵀᴴ OF JUNE

The sauna is warmed up using wood that was sawed and cut by the grandfather, who passed away a few decades ago. The dry wood is crackling silently in the firebox, accompanied by the subtle rumble of the sea. The day is beautiful. Only a few clouds roll slowly by in solitude. Out of nowhere, an inner question indescribable by any mind-made symbols appears. If it were put into words, it would sound like this:

What am I?

The question is not asked through thoughts but conveyed by the essence of being. Ultimately, it is not a question at all, but an answer in the form of wonder. Something deep within it sees itself without any external reference points, without attachment to space or time. The question remains, and the answer arises simultaneously with it. The subtle rumble of the sea and the crackling of the burning wood feel soothing.

It is unclear how long it took for the experience to unveil, as there was no experience of time involved in it. Afterward, it still remains silently rolling in the background, even though most of it disappeared after the climax of the experience. The thoughts remain that most probably triggered the deep state of stillness and exposed the pure awareness of oneself.

Life is full of triggers that lead into deep presence. It seems that this time, the triggers were thoughts concerning time and space. One could intensely feel the grandfather sawing and cutting the wood, and see the trees growing in a forest, and see the young forest full of seedlings of the trees. The smoke rising up to the heavens from the chimney is profoundly interconnected with all those past events.

All space and time happen *'here and now'*. The past and the future, and everything in the farthest corners of the galaxies and the whole universe happen *'here and now'*—in presence. And the essence of that presence is found within every single perspective of existence. Everything and every time happen simultaneously within. The feeling of it carries infinite comfort and benediction. There is not a grain of loss, and one does not lack anything in it. Even though things and forms pass away, a sincere smile remains on the face.

JULY

5TH OF JULY

The inner world is deep and silent this morning. In the ever proceeding experience of time, there is nothing ahead, and through that realization, the past disappears. As the past ceases to exist, the whirlwind of compulsively arising memories also goes. In the heart of every morning, there lingers the vast potential of all that is, springing from the emptiness that gives birth to the whole existence. What could ever be a reason not to accept this potential?

6TH OF JULY

The feeling of presence has deepened. It occurs more often than ever before. It is not initiated in any way, and it is triggered by external events. The feeling cannot be described by thoughts. Thus, it is impossible to convey through words at all. One can only point to the general direction of it with concepts.

A subtle sense of nostalgia is included in the presence. Not a grasping kind of nostalgia, but an appreciative kind. When the presence flows very deep, one feels like crying and tears almost fill the eyes, but at the same time, one feels like laughing. The whole spectrum of emotions unfolds when the feeling of presence is deep. There is no particular reason for the emotions to arise, they just do. The inner tears, combined with boundless yet very subtle joy, is a perfection of the ever-renewing moment of all that is. It is not known conceptually as '*all that is*', but appears as an unknown sensation of totality in one's innermost being.

Today, an unexplainable feeling of loss is accompanied by an experience of regaining. They happen simultaneously, without the smallest gap in time between them. It is not clear what is lost and what is regained, but the happening of it all is evident in everything. It remains a mystery that does not need solving. The mystery unfolds and is recreated in every single moment. It is perfection. Nothing more, and nothing less.

7TH OF JULY

Something forgotten lies beneath the infinite number of objects in the perceivable world. A thick blanket of things covers the vast being inside everything. Consciousness is made manifest every time the being expresses through things, erupting momentarily and ephemerally like lightning in the dark night sky. Everywhere one rests eyes upon acts as a portal to that beingness.

10TH OF JULY

While reading a short scientific text, a curious contemplation arises: the message echoing in the text is only a snapshot of a moment in time, despite it is widely considered as the truth of today. Some time ago, it was not yet the truth, and after a while, it will not be the truth anymore.

The snapshot in time is only a stage in the evolution of things, and things tend to mature out of their stages into new ones, proceeding forever and ever. Nothing stays the same in the realm of time, not even the truths of today. Realizing the inevitably changing nature of existence will reveal the liberation of the soul. The freedom from the unconscious and compulsive mind activities arises in seeing the ephemeral nature of truths.

12TH OF JULY

The river flows slowly. Some waves are created by motorboats. Distant and infrequent sounds of traffic mix with the continuous humming of the flowing water. The sun shines through the leaves of the birch to whose trunk the hammock's other end is tied. The day is beautiful and serene.

The inner serenity opens totally different doors of perception than the normal state of mind. The leaves of the birch seem profoundly green, the flowing of the river sounds crystal clear, and the light breeze feels like a loving embrace of nature herself. The environment is not clouded in any way with the hazy thoughts of compulsive mind activity. No identity remains as the lens of perception. Everything is seen just as it is.

So much of the surrounding world remains unseen when looking through the labeling machinery of the mind. When the mind creates labels, it tends to grasp those labels, and whenever the mind grasps anything, it becomes blind to everything else. When one thinks of something, the mind is taken by the object of the thought. Immersed in the thought-based reality, the true reality is neglected, and one lives in ignorance. Only the stillness within can reveal the depths of this ignorance.

18TH OF JULY

After a long and numbing drive to the north, some mountains rise to the heavens on the horizon. The snow-covered peaks of the giants reflect the rays of the sun perfectly, adding shiny brilliance to their natural whiteness. The mountains' majestic silhouettes against the light blue sky produce a feeling of personal smallness and insignificant youth. However, their sempiternal beingness acts as a bridge to the self within.

The self, who has witnessed the birth of the body and will also see the death of it, has similar sempiternal characteristics as the mountains seem to have. It does not age, and it has always remained the same. It is not affected by time. The self is exactly as full of life as it was when it first became conscious of itself, yet it is as empty as it was before all existence. The absolute nature of the self shines through all the relative expressions of it.

The mind fights against the sensation of something everlasting within. It cannot accept the idea of eternity inside every single grain of awareness. Thus it creates concepts bound in time, explaining rationally how the eternal cannot be. It whispers that if there were something timeless, it must be something a lot greater than a mere human form—something godlike. The mind has a curious habit of putting itself down through rational thinking.

For today, the mind is dismissed. The majestic forms of the mountains are an expression of the majestic form of the inner stillness. The emptiness within prevails. The long drive to the north remains numbing to the body and mind but is now flavored with joyous seeds of unseen eternity.

19TH OF JULY

The air is abnormally warm, but the seawater remains freezing cold. The beach is full of fine white sand, and some shells lie on the waterfront. Small and silent waves wash over them, arriving at the beach serenely one by one, without any haste whatsoever. The coldness of the water makes the feet numb, but standing there is lovable nevertheless. The seafloor is perfectly visible. The water is as clear as water can ever be, and the white grains of sand flow back and forth with the waves of the ocean. The mind becomes crystal clear and transparent like the water.

The waves whisper the secrets of the whole ocean as it takes the form of the waves. Those whispers can be heard in every single sound the waves make when hitting the shoreline, and they can be seen in every little movement of the white grains of sand flowing back and forth. The sand on the seafloor has adopted forms of the water's waves, much like the mind has created its identities. The identities of the mind are but momentary images of the waves of its surroundings. They do not contain real identity, but only forms which shift and change along with the waves.

The children are playing on the beach. They seem to love how the freezing cold water caresses the skin under the scorching sun. The warmth of summer is undeniable, and the snow-covered mountaintops are melting into vast rivers flowing down on the steep faces of the mountains.

21ST OF JULY

The view on top of the fell is breathtaking. The sun still shines, but not very far away a thunderstorm is approaching. The clouds are dark, and they pour down from the sky, caressing the dry nature beneath the rainfall. The heaven sings in thunderous rhythms, even though no lightning is visible. The mind is entirely stopped by the grandeur of nature's play. Everything remains very still even at the edge of the storm.

22ND OF JULY

A dog is barking at the distance. A faint echo of the sound remains for a blink of an eye, and afterward, only the soft rain is heard as it falls on the leaves of the trees and the forest ground. The silence is impenetrable, and not even the occasional cars driving by can break its enchantment. The inner stillness is reflected in the outer silence of nature.

The book feels very light, and almost an unnoticeable scent of the paper flows in the damp air. The letters in the paper seem interesting, locking the gaze for a long time in their myriad, yet limited forms on the white paper. The paper feels rough under the soft fingertips.

A sudden and brief cawing of a crow creates meaning for the deep silence. After some while, the distant sound of thunder echoes in the air. It starts very small, but rapidly the sound grows majestic and penetrates everything in the awareness. Quickly the silence reveals itself again, accompanied by a feeling of unexplainable aliveness.

The stillness within is not a product of an empty mind, but a silence of an open mind. It is the essence of everything, which *is* before any states of mind or forms of matter arise. The silence is not dull or boring but breathes the substance of life itself. Life happens in that silence.

25TH OF JULY

Life is relentless, and the warmth of the summer is undeniable. The barren grass expands in ever wider areas day by day, and there's not even the slightest hint of rain. Only a few lonely clouds move slowly across the open sky. The sun relentlessly watches the entire nature beneath. No wind whatsoever is present, and the air is very still, making the warmth quite much for the body to endure.

Nature seems to be in a quiet power saving mode, and it leads the inner stillness into a clearing inside the forests of the mind. However, the stillness is not and can never be an object of perception. If such a stillness occurs, and if it can be observed, it is not the stillness in that clearing, but a product of the mind's imagination. The mind can produce all kinds of experiences of inner peace and spiritual level-ups, but as long as they can be observed, they are not the self within. The self, which is the essence of the inner stillness, observes, yet it cannot be observed.

Finding the clearing in the forest seems to be a result of a series of awakenings. Time after time, one awakens from unconscious identification of thoughts and other objects, each time in a different way, depending on how different the false identity is at the given moment. The mind's   mechanical   identity-making   machinery continuously grasps different mental positions and creates experiences for those identities. However, no perceivable identity is true and will perish in a matter of time. In the search for oneself, whatever is perceived is not oneself.

26TH OF JULY

Children are blowing soap bubbles. The joy of the play seems unrivaled by anything in the entire world. The unusually warm weather continues, and small gusts of wind carry the bubbles to unexpected directions. The bubble silhouettes against the open blue sky are beautiful, as they dance with the whims of the wind. Their colorful surfaces glimmer in bright colors, changing and shifting. Eventually, they just pop and disappear. Their disappearance happens suddenly and always without warning, even though the bubbles are expected to have short lifespans.

Life is like soap bubbles. Forms appear seemingly out of nowhere, dancing for their time, and then simply and quickly disappear back into nowhere. What is curious about soap bubbles is that their forms are only a surface phenomenon. A bubble is created primarily by the emptiness inside.

AUGUST

1ˢᵀ OF AUGUST

A massive thunderstorm approaches. The air is very still. The warmth of the sun embraces the skin just before it is covered by dark clouds. Nature is silent, and everything is painted with hues of grey. Some birds fly quickly by as the thunder roars in the sky with a power that creates trembles inside the body. The damp and stagnant air creates a stillness, which triggers memories of the freezing cold days of mid-winter.

Life is about balance. Whenever the balance of existence is found, life is found. The balance lingers in every single detail of awareness, in the tiniest things as well as in the massive objects in the vastness of space. The balance is found in relationships, events, thoughts, feelings, emotions, plantlife, inanimate objects, and in everything that can be an object of awareness. Without this balance, existence would not be. Without existence, life would not be.

Life creates existence, and existence creates life. When life is pursued in different ways and forms, more existence is created in different ways and forms. There are no right or wrong forms of existence, but only totalities which establish a perfect balance of rights and wrongs. Those totalities also act as one point of view of vaster patterns of balance. The existence is interdependent, and the balance between the tiniest particle and the most gigantic supercluster of galaxies bears the very essence of existence.

The ultimate balance is found in every form of awareness, where the existent and the non-existent dance together. The dance of existence and utter emptiness is intimate, and there cannot be one without the other. The dance is timeless, and the balance it creates has no boundaries. That balance is the present moment.

4TH OF AUGUST

Listening to the bitter words of a friend. Not many words are spoken, but the bitterness and pain behind them are obvious. The story is short but clear and self-evident. Life has moved on, but the words come from the past. What beautiful joy and glamorous pain can a relationship with another human being produce. The rainfall pounds the windscreen while driving on the motorway. The scenery changes rapidly, and cars come and go.

Life goes on with impeccable certainty. There are different phases in life, with different content in them. If one dwells in a phase which does not exist anymore, suffering arises. One might try to grasp the old and familiar phase of life in the moment of transition, but it will lead only to frustration, which eventually produces more or less suffering. Life will always move forward, regardless of anyone's hopes. The suffering always emerges when hearts are blind and frozen.

5ᵀᴴ OF AUGUST

The older daughter's birthday party creates a lot of fuss today. The preparations take much time, and the anticipation is easily observable in the children's behavior. During the party, the sincere and carefree play of the children mixes with the socializing of the adults, producing a slightly chaotic atmosphere. The occasional heavy rainfalls hammer the roof, and everything seems somewhat hypnotic when stopping to listen to it all.

The noises of the environment act as a portal to inner stillness, no matter how continuous and disturbing they might be. At first, the noise seems to be created by perceivable objects in the surroundings, including people. Then the awareness shifts to space in the room. The chaotic noise turns to a more simple sensation, a deeper sensation, and it becomes very tangible. It seems to have no boundaries. Even the feeling of the movement of the eardrums is one dimension of the noise. When the awareness expands deeper into and toward the perceiver—the one who hears all the noise—the boundaries and limitations of objects disappear completely. All that is left is the hearing of the sound. It does not separate the source of the sound and the one who hears it but the act of hearing happens entirely without separation.

A curious sense of oneness arises. The party goes on, but the environment feels a lot simpler than it was just a moment ago. Not simple as a conceptual idea, but simple as the existence in itself.

6TH OF AUGUST

The inner stillness always comes in darkness. It never comes through invitation. If any force is exercised, even the smallest of thought or action, then the result is only more force—force always means limitation. All kinds of spiritual experiences, even the most wonderful ones, can happen through force, but true stillness cannot be achieved by force. The inner stillness cannot be attained by thwarting reality through thoughts of becoming.

The curse of the human mind is that it is always in a vicious loop of becoming. All actions reflect that loop, and therefore becoming anything can never bestow unlimited liberation. All becoming is based on the small and limited 'I' within the mind, which seeks to be something else than it is, which seeks to turn the world to something else than it is. When one sees the 'I' who applies force in becoming, the limitedness of the 'I' is seen. It is seen by no-one in particular because the inner stillness always comes in darkness.

What already is, cannot be invited. The only reality, where liberation resides, is found only in *what is.* The act of inviting already is that. When one seeks for the inner stillness and the liberation of the mind, one actually perceives from the inner stillness. It is something that cannot be revealed nor found because it is already revealed and found.

9TH OF AUGUST

It has rained during the night. While walking toward the office, the rising sun shines in a perfect angle to reflect the blinding light from the surface of the wet street. The street is a shining golden bridge in which dark silhouettes of people flow quite peacefully.

10TH OF AUGUST

Walking through the narrow forest road with the dog. The sound of the strong wind blowing through the leaves carries wordless words with it. The raging sea sings its song in the background while proceeding deeper into the peace of the living forest—the peace within. Utter stillness resides in the forest even though the trees are bending in the wind and the overall noise is quite powerful.

11TH OF AUGUST

The wind roars, and the waves crest in the sea. They hit the shoreline with astounding power. The water is high, and the whole beach is covered in rumbling waves. The big rock one spent a long time standing on yesterday is now beneath the opaque surface of the debris-filled water. The sky is grey, and only a few openings in the clouds over the sea occasionally let sunlight through. On such passing moments, the sea temporarily becomes molten gold, waving ever closer with its never-ending beauty. Everything is embraced by the incessant humming of the moving masses of air, and the trees bend with powerful gusts of wind.

Slowly, a sense of identity is replaced with an inner stillness. There is no one standing on the stormy beach, but only unity of the mind, body, sea, and the roaring wind. The clothes are flapping in the continuous blowing of the wind, and small drops of seawater from the cresting waves feel refreshing on the skin. Oneness of the experiences is felt, and only the peacefulness of the storm prevails. There is no effort whatsoever in attaining the peace, but it has emerged as a consequence of the ceasing of all effort.

No movement of the mind is present, which would try to grasp the inner peace. The mind is silent and still, but it is not empty and dull. Some thoughts pass by, arising

162

and falling like the cresting waves in the sea. The thoughts, however, do not devour the awareness but evaporate the same way they appeared in the first place—from nothingness to nothingness.

The wind keeps on roaring. The waves keep on coming. In the center of it all, one stands unchanging and unmoving.

13TH OF AUGUST

The younger daughter holds a book in her hands, with an excited look on her face. The book tells a story of one of the most horrific calamities in the known history, but all she talks about is the picture of a withered leaf on the cover of the book; she thinks it is a magic leaf, which bestows inherent abilities for flying. There is no hint of thought concerning the actual message in the book and the cover. How could there be, as there is no knowledge of it all?

Children are beautifully oblivious to such things, which affect adults' lives. They do not know the psychological pain and suffering in the same way, and they do not carry around redundant stories which amplify the pain and suffering.

However, the adults normally adopt mental positions that hinder the children in their boundless being. Adults create restrictions to be honored, requirements to be fulfilled, and knowledge to be learned. The kingdom of heaven is within a child's reach, but too often the adults forcefully stuff the child's mind with redundant knowledge.

Redundant knowledge always creates obstacles to see oneself.

14TH OF AUGUST

Awakening from the strangest dream quite early in the morning. The family is still asleep. The dream was sequential, and in every sequence, one was an entirely different person. The lives of those persons intertwined in some hidden and unknown way, and even though those persons did not know that, something within them knew. Something that was the same in each one of them.

There is something within all sentient beings which connects them in the deepest of ways—a way words cannot convey. The closest thing that could describe it is to call it the *sense of self*. It is the sense of self without any ideas or concepts attached to it, which has no meaning, yet it definitely is. It might not emerge in the same way in every being; some feel like individual selves, and some feel more attuned to collective selves, or somewhere in the middle. But the only thing true, pristine, and unchanging in every single being is, that the *sense of self* is there.

A sense of self is not an identity. It is not a personality. It is not the mind, nor the body. Thinking cannot grasp it. It is revealed only when all grasping ceases. And this is immeasurably difficult for the human mind; to cease all grasping. The habit of grasping goes very deep, and even the most seemingly spiritual person might be as much submerged in a dream of grasping and attachment as anyone else. Only different ways of grasping occur, and in almost all human beings, the behavior is so hidden that even trying to get hold of it is quite impossible.

When all grasping, becoming and identifying cease, the 'sense of self' emerges. This emergence does not hold any promises within.

15ᵀᴴ OF AUGUST

Lying on the terrace sofa after a surgical operation. Some pain is present, but nothing the body can not handle. The sun shines from the open sky. The air is very still and warm. The aspen trees' seeds dance in the air without a destination. The small, fluffy, and white parachutes look like little diamonds as the rays of the sun shine through them.

Nothing more beautiful exists at the moment. The seeds' dance is a dance of perfection, where every single movement reflects the entire dance. There is no dancer. Only the dance and all its tiny parts shine in the light of the awareness. Also, nothing is aware of the dance. Only the awareness exists, and nothing more. Utter peace and stillness soothe the body and mind. The pain in the body is very much present, but whatever is present at any time or any place, merges with the timeless peace within.

16TH OF AUGUST

The daughters push the limits like all small children sometimes do. The pain in the body after the surgical operation is still present, and some agitated feelings arise. The mind thinks the situation holds some massive unbalance, as the agitated feelings merge with the purposefully irritating behavior of the offspring.

Suddenly, without warning, the mind's deeply unconscious state of denial is relinquished. The illusory unbalance of the situation is instantly replaced by a deep feeling of a perfect balance. Without thoughts or words, a realization arises, how the agitated feelings and the children's behavior complete each other. As a result of the realization, all resistance against the situation disappears.

The feelings are still present, but the state of being turns to utter peace and total awareness of the situation. The stillness within holds no expectations or promises for the situation to clear up, but nevertheless, it slowly starts doing so. The inner peace and stillness start to reflect gradually in the external situation.

The balance of everything remains as it ever was—perfect.

19TH OF AUGUST

The state of denial the mind usually lingers in is breathtaking. It incessantly dwells somewhere else than in the present moment. The mind's illusory reality shows only deficient images of what has been, what is, and what will be. Often it offers images of what has never been, and what will never be. Those images deny the existence of 'here and now'.

Whenever the mind believes it is present, it is actually filled with labels and concepts representing what is. It might even trick itself with a peaceful experience of presence, or even a spiritual experience, but what actually echoes in the mind is the belief of being present. The state of denial is deep and unconscious. The denial leads to resistance, and resistance always produces more or less suffering. It might occur as a peaceful experience at the moment, but the nature of all experience is oscillation.

The sky is filled with clouds that look like snow-covered mountaintops. They are everywhere, and their collective shape is very symmetrical. Small openings of the blue sky are seen in regular patterns between the white mountaintops. The greyish lower portion of the curtain of clouds seems like it was cut off, and they seem to be resting on an invisible layer of nothingness. A distant sound of a helicopter reaches the ears, as it flies over the cloudy horizon.

21ST OF AUGUST

Resting in inner stillness, embraced by the flux of the world. There are things to do, words to say, people to meet, opinions to be expressed, truths to be uttered, something

167

to leave behind, and something to become, but nothing can tremble the ground on which one stands.

22ND OF AUGUST

The mornings are getting colder already. The crisp air brings the first sensations of the coming autumn, but the slowly rising sun still bears memories of the warmth of summer. Long shadows stretch on the backyard. In the areas where the sunlight meets the ground, the morning dew makes the lawn glimmer like it was made of a multitude of small bright crystals, reflecting the light in most beautiful colors.

There is no sense of hurry, even though the children must be taken to the school and daycare in time. The mind is as peaceful as the shining crystals on the lawn, but a barely unobservable distortion is felt. There is something illusory included in the inner peace—an imaginary emptiness. It is a manufactured emptiness, a deeply hidden state of the mind.

An empty mind is not a sign of the *self* within, but only a state of the mind that can be observed. It produces a sense of presence that is at best an ephemeral experience. It is one of the myriad faces in the play of life that leads to unconsciously identifying with the state of the mind. It is a simulacrum of liberation the mind dreams about, but never attains permanently.

There seems to be no way out. The mind is a snake eating its own tail. The tools of the mind cannot solve the structure of the mind because they are an intrinsic part of the mind. The futility of all effort in changing becomes crystallized. Realizing this brings about a sudden wave of anxiety, but at the same time, the familiar feeling of true liberation arises.

This liberation carries no identities and no illusory images of being or becoming something. The deep inner peace sensed by the mind is replaced by something indescribable, but what shines through all the false experiences of inner peace. A clenched spiritual fist opens and relaxes, and the need for all control vanishes.

It all happens seemingly because of one wordless realization, which is forgotten over and over again, and remembered over and over again:

Something is aware of the ephemeral states of the mind.

That something is always aware of everything, including the false state of the inner peace. And to be more precise, it is not even something because when looked for, it cannot be found. It is formless awareness and empty stillness.

The familiar dialogue with the daughters continues even though the realization happens. Liberation is not an act of getting out, but more of a way of getting into the world. First, the older daughter goes to school, then the younger to the daycare, and afterward, the journey continues toward the office.

With the realization, nothing has changed, but everything shines like small diamonds in the all-encompassing awareness, that belongs to no one.

SEPTEMBER

4ᵀᴴ OF SEPTEMBER

Awake in the middle of the night. The family is asleep, and the house is dark and quiet. The machinery of the mind is mostly silent. Only some random thoughts run through the mind, with memories of yesterdays and expectations of tomorrows. A distant sound of a car driving by is heard, but it quickly fades away into the silence of the night. Some time passes before getting up.

Night-time is intriguing. The whole world is asleep, and there is mostly silence, which penetrates everything in existence. The streetlamps shine through the curtains, creating an immovable and eerie dance of faint light and deep shadows. The sky is clouded. No stars are visible, and there is no sign of the moon at all. The silence in the house is intense, and the silent darkness creates a soothing feeling of anticipation of the coming winter.

5ᵀᴴ OF SEPTEMBER

The mornings are getting slightly colder, and the body needs time to adapt to the colder air. It feels very chilling already, even though the temperature is not that low yet. Small shivers go through the body as the cool wind embraces everything with a subtle, yet all-encompassing touch. The sun rises slowly, and there is no warmth to its beautiful rays yet.

Adapting to the surroundings is often the key out of suffering, either physical or mental. The ability to adapt is the key to life itself. The mind is prone to resist things that cause pain and suffering, but if the situation already produces pain and suffering, there is no need to resist them. However, it does not mean disregarding the feelings, it only means disregarding the inner resistance which arises in unpleasant situations. There is no point whatsoever to resist what already is.

Mental adaptation might need some time, just like the body needs time to adapt to the colder climate. The adaptation will happen instantaneously if no resistance against the situation arises. The time needed to adapt to a given situation is only dependent on the time the mind thinks it needs. Time is the mind's playground and its natural habitat. Inner peace and stillness reveal timelessness, in which no resistance can arise. That

174

timeless dimension of being reveals the perfection that already resides within.

Accompanying the older daughter on the way to school. The first year at school is one of the important moments of adaptation in life, and the daughter seems to accept the adaptation with a curious smile on her face.

6TH OF SEPTEMBER

Some stress and anxiety are present. The mind repeats worried thoughts over and over again. It is evident how conditioned behavior usually triggers when facing mental or physical stress. Trying to fight the stress only empowers it.

Suddenly, in a deep moment of anxiety, while uttering tempered words, a feeling of waking from hypnosis with the snap of the fingers emerges. Instantly, an unjudging awareness sheds light on all those worrying thoughts, as well as the inner struggle with the anxiety. The compulsively pouring thoughts cease to exist at the very moment the awareness emerges, and as the *effect* of one's own experience relinquishes, they instead become the *cause* of one's own experience. The circumstance is no more prior to the awareness, but the awareness arises before the circumstance. There are actions, but no reactions. The conscious experience of life emerges.

The mind's fundamental nature is confinement. Whatever the mind thinks about external things, is only an expression of the current state of mind, and does not say anything about the external things. A confession of love for another human being does not say anything about the another but expresses only the state of the confessing mind. Hateful words do not say anything about the object of the hate but are merely an expression of the hostility the speaker carries within.

There is nothing one can do to make changes in oneself or the world. All change is a product of the level of consciousness one holds within. The question is not *what* can be done, but *how* aware one is of oneself. Through simply being aware, changes start occurring in the surrounding world.

7TH OF SEPTEMBER

To see perfection in another human being is to know the completeness of oneself.

8TH OF SEPTEMBER

The evening sky is like a watercolor painting. The light blue sky reflects from the still surface of the sea, and only some subtle ripples are seen here and there, as the light wind blows from the west. The sea merges into the deep red sunset in the horizon, and the whole view slowly fades into the blueness of the sky through hues of orange and yellow. The trees on the beach are immovable. Their dark green silhouettes in the withdrawing sunlight look like statues carved from pure stillness. Only occasionally do the leaves of the trees tremble in the gentle embrace of the wind, but their movement is very subtle, seeming almost illusory; the trees certainly move, but when perceived, they are utterly still.

The stillness of the surrounding air and the serenity of the sea view bring forth the familiar sensation of inner stillness. It is not an experience, as all experience is time-bound, but a timeless state of being indescribable by words. The mind and body are deeply affected by the recognition of that stillness. Deep inner peace and unconditional happiness overwhelm the unity of the mind and body.

Slowly the sun sets below the horizon. The deep orange bridge it paints on the surface of the sea slowly fades into the dark waters. The air turns colder the very instant the sun disappears, and the unity of the mind and body decides to go back to the warmth of the house. The stillness within remains for the rest of the evening.

11TH OF SEPTEMBER

The identity tends to get interested in other identities, that seem to possess something it does not have itself. That is why stories of transcendence in other people's histories are so appealing. The identity also finds alluring the stories that someone tells about other people's transcendent experiences. Stories that include something of value to gain and to reach for, attract the mind like a magnet. However, stories are ephemeral. They do not define oneself, and they are not oneself. The 'I' within every mind is only a vague set of selected memories and filtered stories. The self is the space in which all those stories arise and fall.

12TH OF SEPTEMBER

Deep gratitude emerges while walking toward the office. The gratitude is sensed in the cool air as the soft drizzle caresses the skin. It is seen in the tiny drops of water hanging from the tips of the pine needles. Those drops reflect an entire universe inside them in perfectly round shapes. The gratitude is heard in children's laughter on a nearby schoolyard and the distant noise of the motorway. It is felt in the heartbeats and the rough feeling of gravel under the feet. It is seen in the green lawns, the withered leaves, the colorful flowers, and the dried ponds. Everywhere the awareness travels, the gratitude is there waiting, as it has always been.

Nothing obstructs the peaceful sense of gratitude, even though some thoughts arise describing all the tasks that must be taken care of. The difference to a normal state of unconscious mind activity is that pure awareness embraces every single thought arising. The unconscious mind always becomes the thoughts it bears within after the thoughts have arisen, but now it feels like the awareness exists before the thinking mind. As a result, no sense of identity is derived from thoughts.

Being the cause of one's own creations is the core of all gratitude and unconditional love. It is the natural state, which is found beyond the compulsively thinking mind. In this natural state, the body and mind relax, creating space for things to be just as they are. All things are beautiful just as they are.

14ᵀᴴ OF SEPTEMBER

The morning is chilly. The cool wind feels penetrating on the skin. The rising sun paints the roofs of the buildings with bright colors, but mostly everything below the roofs is still covered in the morning twilight. It has rained during the night. Some yellow leaves have fallen from the branches of the birch trees, and they lie immovable on the wet lawn. The inevitable signs of autumn are seen everywhere.

The mind is puzzled this morning. Inner silence is deep, and awareness of the surroundings is impenetrable. However, the mind continually tries to grasp and cling to the inner silence, trying to understand it. It seems to think that understanding the stillness within leads to miraculous results and all the promises the idea of enlightenment holds.

The problem of the mind's search for enlightenment is that it thinks the emptiness is a thing and an object in awareness. However, what is nothing cannot be an object of awareness—it is not called *no-thing* in vain. The emptiness is beyond perception, and therefore beyond understanding. The mind can never grasp it. The thing called emptiness can act as a gateway to emptiness within, but it can also lead one far astray. Whenever the thing called emptiness arises, the best one can do is to remain aware of oneself. It is the only way to liberation.

15ᵀᴴ OF SEPTEMBER

The forest is filled with colors of light green and yellow, as nature starts preparing for winter. The sound of the wind blowing through the leaves of the trees rise and fall like waves in an ocean. Every time it rises, some bright yellow leaves hover slowly down to the ground. There is no hurry whatsoever, and everything happens precisely on time. The forest's yielding to the coming winter is beautiful, even though it means a long period of slumber and death.

Every time the waves of the wind sink into the trough, the whole world is rendered magnificently quiet. No sounds of the city's constant background noise stain the serenity of the deep forest. The peacefulness of nature becomes tangible in the simple act of perception. To find inner stillness, one only has to look around. However, there can be no expectation of finding inner stillness. If such an expectation is present, one is already engulfed by the machinery of the mind. The mind cannot acquire inner peace, but can only find temporary reflections of that peace—temporary things that seem to bestow peaceful experiences.

The mind continuously seeks ever more growing needs and illusory expectations. Only when one becomes truly aware of the mind's constant effort to acquire inner peace does one suddenly find oneself standing outside the fortress of the mind. It can happen only in the present moment and pure awareness.

A small white butterfly appears out of nowhere. The contrast it creates against the green forest is an image of perfection. It slowly makes its way toward unknown places, accepting totally the occasional gusts of wind that throw it off balance, and then it proceeds again as if nothing serious has happened. Life has a strong tendency to shrug off any imbalance very quickly and proceed in its way without second thoughts—without regrets or worries.

16TH OF SEPTEMBER

The clear starry sky above breathes the very essence of the universe. The stars seem like little diamonds scattered over an infinitely deep emptiness, glowing in the empowering light of the existence itself. Even trying to think about the distance between those beautiful diamonds makes the mind stop. Such distances cannot be comprehended by the mind but on a very shallow conceptual level. The stillness of the glimmering dark sky is a portrait of serenity and perfect balance, where discord at one level seems like harmony on the other level.

The campfire is crackling, and the dance of the flames feels hypnotic in the growing darkness of the late evening. There are no limitations to the dance, and it never stops—not even for a fraction of a second. The fire creates a sphere of light embraced by the deep forest, and whatever hides there beyond the light, remains unknown.

The sensation of total unknowing deepens the stillness within, singing the same song of serenity with the immovable sky filled with shining diamonds.

A nearby river hums peacefully. Its constant whispering is like the dance of the flames; it cannot be controlled, it has no limits, and it is different in each moment. A magnificent, yet subtle oneness with the surrounding nature is sensed, and there is no need for control of the situation. The deep-rooted need for control which arises along with the first signs of identity in the human mind is entirely absent. With the absence of that primal need, one's identity cannot be found anywhere. Identity does not exist, when the need for control does not exist. As they are both gone, there is also no suffering of any kind. Suffering has a curious tendency to disappear with the disappearance of identity.

18TH OF SEPTEMBER

The human mind is a complex mechanism of abstractions. It harbors illusory images of what other people are, and additionally, it considers what other people think of itself. Thus, one seems to behave in the way one thinks others think about oneself. Both those images and thoughts are illusory. The identity created by those illusions does not exist. For the thinking mind, it is impossible to accept that the identity would be an illusion. For the silent mind, it is evident.

Talking and writing about the problematic state of the compulsively thinking human mind makes the hearers and readers anxious. They withdraw even more into the fortress of the mind, protecting something they think is precious. A deep reluctance to face itself lingers in the foundations of the false identity.

20TH OF SEPTEMBER

The lightning storm rumbles deeply early in the morning. The family is still asleep, but the children seem restless in their sleep with the thundering sky. The lightning flashes behind the window blinds, accompanied by the deep roaring sounds of thunder. A sense of primal awe is felt every time lightning strikes somewhere near, and in that awe is an impenetrable emptiness full of life.

26TH OF SEPTEMBER

The view opening in the hotel room's window is peaceful. The morning is early, and the sun is just about to rise. The first rays of the morning sunlight paint the roofs of the buildings with golden light. The reflections of the light dance on the opposite building's walls, which are still covered by the slowly waning darkness of the night. In the distance, some flags move wildly with the intense wind, yet with an elegance of a waving ocean. Only a few people walk on the street, and their pace seems peaceful.

It is interesting how everything seems peaceful when observed from a distance. When far enough, objects appear to be almost still and fade into an impossibly small space called nothing. As one perceives the world a bit closer, the world tends to disperse into ever tinier and more chaotic pieces, interacting with each other like the waves in the ocean. The mind itself feels closer than anything else can ever get, and its chaotic nature is evident.

29TH OF SEPTEMBER

The forest ground is covered in white frost. Nature seems very still and quiet. The colors of the forest are quickly waning, but there are still autumn colors seen everywhere around; shades of deep red, light orange, and bright yellow, mixed with the evergreen hues of spruces. Some trees seem as if they were on fire, as the flame-colored leaves shiver in the light northern breeze. Bright yellow leaves occasionally fall to the ground like they were raining from the sky. Everything is filled with the rising sun's light.

The air is cold, and the vapor of the breath is clearly seen before it disappears into the surrounding air. The crisp weather whispers silent words of change, as whole nature welcomes the coming winter heartily. Even the fell seems to emit more silence than ever before, as it bathes in the golden sunlight that sheds forgiveness with each and every one of its rays. Some snow rests on top of the fell, creating just a bit of whiteness on which the morning light can reflect.

A couple of Siberian jays land on a nearby tree. Their landing is quiet and elegant, and if one were not looking at the general direction of them, one would not have seen them arriving. The birds sit there on a branch of big spruce, slowly moving their wings, and basking in the sunlight that just barely lights the treetops.

Everything is quiet. All is blissfully meaningless. Meaningless in a way that allows life to breathe freely, without imposing any judgments or labels on anything. No ignorance or dullness of the mind is experienced, but a precise awareness without any thoughts staining its purity and oneness. That awareness blows life into the ever continuing cycle of birth and death in nature.

OCTOBER

3TH OF OCTOBER

Again the morning is cold. The lawn on the backyard is covered in white frost, and the whole yard glimmers like it were covered with a thousand diamonds in the morning sunlight. The rays of the sun light up the hedgerow in the back of the yard and the yellow leaves seem to bathe in the perfection of all the light in the heavens. All the leaves seem exaggeratedly three-dimensional; their details are seen exceptionally precisely. It is as if their perfection lingered somewhere else than the three dimensions of space and outside time as well. But the curious experience passes very quickly, becoming just a memory in the endless vortices of the mind.

Some anxiety is present this morning. The mind rages about a multitude of things. It is incessant and suffocates any feelings of inner peace. Despite its suffocating behavior, it tries to get rid of the behavior itself, creating a never-ending loop of suffocating and trying. The tragedy of the human mind is that it is blind to its own productions. At one moment it is a portrait of anxiety, and at another moment it is a portrait of trying to get rid of anxiety. The mind changes as fast as one thinks.

There are moments of no thought, during which the anxiety disappears. It seems the anxiety is intrinsic in anxious thoughts only, and otherwise, it is absent. In the same way, the false identity—which feels the anxiety—is actually intrinsic in thoughts and does not exist when thoughts cease happening. With the awareness of the constantly changing nature of the mind, compassion for oneself emerges.

The mind-made sense of identity is a hollow prison, in which one can only scratch the walls, making them look like different walls. But the walls remain the same forever and ever. Only after realizing the suffocating nature of the mind, and that nothing can be done to change it, one suddenly finds oneself existing outside the prison. True freedom can be obtained only by realizing that no thought can really describe true freedom.

4TH OF OCTOBER

The day has been insanely busy, both at work and at home. Relaxing in the sauna. As the hiss of the evaporating water ceases on the sauna stove, a sudden emptiness is felt inside everything: the scoop holding the water, hands, body, and the warm embrace of the sauna. It is not emptiness in a negative and meaningless way, but a stillness experienced in a very fulfilling way. This emptiness holds life in it and nothing else.

There is no one in the body, and no one aware of everything happening, but yet, there is awareness of everything. This dichotomy feels paradoxical, and thinking about it does not make any sense at all. All that can be done is to yield to the feeling, become peaceful with it, and let the oneness emerge.

There is no experience of someone separate feeling the feeling of oneness. There is no experience of someone being aware of anything. Only oneness and awareness remains. No one lies down in the warm sauna, but only warmth and the body that provides the feeling of warmth are sensed. It is as if layers of perception were removed entirely, leaving only the direct experience of perception. In that directness, the inner stillness prevails.

5TH OF OCTOBER

Taking the daughters to school and daycare. The darkness of the night slowly recedes as the sun rises on the horizon. As the first rays of the sun lighten the treetops, the gloomy rainfall suddenly turns into a light snowfall. The rain that was just seconds ago falling straight toward the ground slowly transforms into slowly hovering whiteness. In a matter of few breaths, the rainfall has turned into a full-fledged snowfall.

Change of form is one of the most impressive things in existence. It is seen everywhere in nature, as well as in the experience called human life. All things change, and whatever resistance there is against the change will produce suffering. Clinging to the ideas of the past is like a snowflake trying to turn itself back into a raindrop, even though the climate has already turned to freezing cold. Resistance cannot bring back the past, but acceptance will open doors to the present moment filled with immeasurable love and openness. Not in a poetic way, but in a very tangible way.

Gazing wistfully as the older daughter strolls through the schoolyard, her small profile diminishing in the distance, and eventually disappearing behind the corner of the school building. The snow hovers peacefully to the ground. Some snowflakes land on the face, while still gazing at the empty space where the older daughter's profile had just been. After a short silence, the younger daughter then exclaims: "The water is snowing!" The wistfulness within turns to acceptance and the acceptance turns to inner joy and happiness. All joy in life is about being aware of the present moment. All change in life is about letting go.

6TH OF OCTOBER

The false sense of identity feels endangered whenever the inner stillness grows deeper. Resistance arises. The thought "What if I'm wrong?" appears as the mind tries to resort to conceptual knowledge, desperately clinging to the world of names and symbols. With such behavior, the false sense of identity called the 'I' tries to cling to itself; it is a pattern of symbolic thoughts trying to cling to other patterns of symbolic thoughts. What the mind cannot see in the process is that whatever is named, is part of a nameless process, an existence happening every time and everywhere in one undivided moment—the presence within.

Existence called existence is not existence. The 'I' called the 'I' is not the self, but a lifeless set of symbols. Life is seen when perceiving the world beyond the veil of blinding symbols.

In a world where *everything* has a nameless source—including the names that are given to myriad things—there cannot be anything wrong. Trusting the inner stillness and the nameless emptiness within can never be wrong as it is the source of existence. The mind fights against it, plunging deeper into a dream of names and labels, deeper into the illusion of knowledge. The illusion of knowledge is the source of all intellectual arrogance. Today, deep compassion is felt for the mind and its constantly struggling nature.

8TH OF OCTOBER

The incessant pouring of thoughts cannot be stopped. It is impossible with the tools of the mind. Only after realizing this and yielding humbly to that realization does the mind actually stop. Nothing can be done to stop the mind, and it is impossible to *do nothing* because trying to do nothing is *doing something*. Therefore, truly doing nothing—spontaneously ceasing all doing—is the only way to silence the mind. 'Doing nothing' is to die for oneself, and when death occurs without perishing, life will endure.

9TH OF OCTOBER

The thing called 'awakening' feels like stretching a rubber band. As one becomes more awake, the mind starts pouring thoughts more. As a result, one becomes more aware of the hidden activities of the mind. This, in turn, boosts the awareness of the deeper self.

10TH OF OCTOBER

Life is many times like dancing on beautiful roses, but every once in a while, one steps on the thorns. There has not been much sleep during the night because the younger daughter has a severe flu with a fever. Additionally, the older daughter vomits all night. The mind whispers how spiritual awakening is more difficult for a parent, as there are so many responsibilities and things parents have to take care of. However, the mind can only describe the world of the mind. In that world, finding the peace of mind can indeed be more difficult for parents than for anyone else.

When perceiving the world beyond the mind, it is clearly seen that the awakening is no more difficult for anyone than anyone else. The awakening is already within every sentient being. The only thing that differs is the conscious awareness of it, and even when the unconsciousness runs deep, it is actually the awakening experiencing itself unconsciously. One cannot get rid of it, no matter how one's life is lived. To be even more precise with words, life is not something that can be lived. Life can only be, and it is not something that someone does, or goes through. Life is constant.

No less life is experienced in the middle of the night while helping the older daughter to vomit. Some tiredness and tension of the mind and body are present, but even when occasionally stepping on the thorns in the elegant dance of life, some stillness within is felt. In that stillness, life flourishes. It does so in bad times, as well as in good times.

11TH OF OCTOBER

A good night's sleep again. The body feels revitalized. The weather is grey outside, and serenity pulses through the greyness. No sign of the sun is seen, even though it's already late morning. A peek out of the terrace door reveals it is quite warm outside. The air feels damp as if it was starting to rain very soon. The daughters are getting better already as the diseases loosen their grip on their small bodies.

It is magnificent in children how, even when they are very sick, they never lose their natural softness, and they show their weakness directly, without any shame connected to it. This is profoundly different from an adult mind, which is mostly stiff and strong. Whatever is stiff will break in time. Whatever is strong will weaken in time. Whoever is like children, regaining the natural softness and flexibility of the mind and body from moment to moment, without having to exercise any force in doing so, will express pure life in them.

12TH OF OCTOBER

The sky is grey, and the weather is damp and unusually warm. Despite the overall greyness of the sky, a curious-looking small area above reveals bright blue, as if something had just penetrated the thick layer of otherwise impenetrable greyness. Inside that area, a few distant white clouds drift slowly by, shining in the endless rays of the sun. The scenery is astounding, and the opening seems like a portal to another dimension.

In life, whenever anxiety and greyness prevail, such portals can be found. One can see them only if attention is given to them. It means letting go of one's negative feelings even for a fraction of a second. Negative feelings are nothing that has to be held on to, but ephemeral phenomena in the ocean of rising and falling feelings. They are unconsciously held precious and cherished by the mind. Additionally, the mind normally tries to get rid of the negative feelings, ending up only in deepening them. They deepen because the mind tries to get rid of itself, which is impossible.

Whenever the mind stops, a bright blue portal is created in the impenetrable greyness, letting eternal light shine through into the world of the mind. Such portals appear spontaneously in the present moment. They shine relief and inner stillness through them.

13ᵀᴴ OF OCTOBER

The unusual warmness of the weather still continues. The sun shines brightly, painting the yellow leaves lying on the ground with a shimmering golden aura. The leaves crunch softly under the feet as the family walks toward the car. Last scents of late summer float in the air, mixed with the delightfully withering feelings of autumn and the subtle anticipation of the coming winter. The daughters are curiously quiet and calm, unlike how children usually are. They too probably wonder about the magnificent colors of nature.

While driving back home, light gusts of wind occasionally blow more yellow leaves from the trees. The falling leaves shine in the glorious rays of the sun like thousand vibrating angels were dancing on the road ahead. The familiar stillness within reveals itself as the car proceeds through the painfully beautiful yellow rain. The presence of stillness is not felt as an experience, but deep within, it occurs in the crossing of the experience and the experiencer. The stillness *is* the deeper self, which is not abstract in any way, yet impossible to describe with any kind of concepts. The stillness is the space for all experiences to happen, just like space is needed for the rain of the thousand yellow leaves to happen.

14TH OF OCTOBER

The mind is a machinery of abstractions. Abstract thinking bestows the human mind an ability to imagine things that don't even exist. It is a blessing, as well as a curse. The mind thinks non-existent things as real, and thus it is prone to live in a world which does not exist. In doing so, one forgets the deeper self.

19TH OF OCTOBER

A barren-looking birch tree stands alone against the grey sky. All the leaves have withered and dropped, yet the tree radiates some unknown but very distinct kind of life. The existence of the tree and its crude form against the colorless sky are undeniable, and it flows in the same stillness that flows within oneself. Nothing exists, which would be separate from this stillness. It is the source of inexhaustible energy.

Existence is an infinite flow of energy, which takes myriad forms *'here and now'*, echoing the essence of one's innermost being. This being *is* the existence, as well as the stillness and emptiness, which give rise to existence. Whatever there is, and whenever anything happens, is a product of inner emptiness reflecting in a seemingly external world. However, paradoxically, there are no inner and outer worlds—the source of all life is one.

The form of the barren tree against the grey sky is the source, just like everything in existence is the source of existence. Whatever exists, is a beautiful perfection of this source of infinite emptiness of infinities.

21ˢᵀ OF OCTOBER

The darkness is as impenetrable as the silence. It is freezing, and the breath is seen clearly in the air just before it evaporates into the surrounding darkness. Some distant barking of dogs is heard, and they echo in the still air in an eerie way. Even though it is cold, no snow covers the ground, making the landscape even darker.

Standing on the porch after a long drive to the north, listening to the silence and gazing the stars above. Everything is remarkably still. Some occasional sounds arise from the silence, only to return to the silence after a short while. No background noise of a city is heard, and the silence feels deeply soothing. The darkness and silence open a portal into inner silence.

The fell's dark silhouette is barely seen in the distance. The mind feels just like the silhouette of the fell—it is distant, and its profile merges into the surrounding emptiness. The mind cherishes all the sensory perceptions of the body, but their importance is next to nothing in the deep infinity of the surrounding emptiness. The mind holds no true importance of any kind. What is important is the sense of being in the present moment. Aligning with the present moment without any personal history is of true importance.

23RD OF OCTOBER

The mind includes multiple layers of awareness, but none of them is really transcendent. The mind can only be aware of itself; the perceived layers of awareness happen in the mind, only extending outward from it. The mind cannot escape its own inherent limitations, and when it notices that, it becomes frustrated. In the wake of frustration, many dark things arise.

While sitting in the warm sauna after a long hike in nature, the chain reactions of the mind are evident. First, the mind conjures thoughts blindly and unconsciously, like in a dream. No awareness of being in the dream is present, as the dream is all that exists. Then, the mind notices how the automatic streams of thought arise in that dream, and the mind becomes the state of noticing. However, what is actually noticed are the previous thoughts that belong to the past. There is no transcendence in thinking and being aware of the past, even if it was only a few seconds ago. After that, the mind finds out that it is impossible to escape the mind, and immediately it becomes a portrait of frustration. In that frustration, a subtle feeling of suffering is sensed.

No matter how aware the mind strives to become, it can at most express the conditioned state of itself, and nothing more. In its lonely prison, the mind needs compassionate guidance.

No transcended, enlightened, or awakened mind or identity can exist. Whatever those words point to, can happen only in the absence of compulsive thinking and the disintegration of the false identity. True transcendence is literally nothing we can think of, and nothing that can be achieved. It seems impossible for the mind to understand this.

24TH OF OCTOBER

The thin layer of ice covers the 'saivo', one of the mystical and sacred lakes of the ancient people. The water underneath the icy surface is breathtakingly clear. The lake floor can be seen through the ice as it plunges down into the darkness very steeply. In the edge of that impenetrable darkness, a white trunk of a fallen birch tree glows eerily, lying on the lake floor. The stillness of the 'saivo' is as deep as the lake goes, and the mind cannot grasp its deepness. It is covered in still and dark waters, and an immovable layer of ice reflects everything that happens above. It quickly becomes evident how the ancient people have found this lake sacred—it emits distinct sacredness and inner stillness in just being there.

There is no time to stay with the lake for a very long time, as the daughters are eager to move forward on the forest path. Even though only a short time of inner stillness is present, it feels timeless. The spaciousness of it is as deep as the waters below the lake's surface. There is no observable end to it.

29TH OF OCTOBER

Still no snow, but the air is freezing cold. The whole world is covered in bleak hues of frost, and the crispness of the air caresses the skin. The breath evaporates into the surrounding coldness, and everything is just as clear as the sky is. The half-moon is unusually bright above, even though the darkness of night has already faded away.

The world happens in a very peaceful way this morning. The absence of movement is very tangible; no birds or animals are seen, no clouds obstruct the beautiful sky, the air carries no smells, and everything is peaceful and quiet. The peacefulness of the surrounding world and the absence of the experience of movement reveals the familiar sense of stillness within. Even though movement is perceived in that stillness, it is not experienced as movement, but rather a surface phenomenon, like the surface of a vast ocean. The surface can be sensed, but it does not exist in any way the mind could understand. The surface of the ocean is an infinitesimal plane dividing a bottomless ocean and an eternal sky.

What could be more blissful than to be such an ocean and sky while alive? Life happens in between two peaceful eternities. Nothing can compete with the magnificence of that experience.

30ᵀᴴ OF OCTOBER

The *self* is so all-encompassing that one cannot miss it once starting to search for it. However, it might take some time and detours before the realization occurs through experience:

The self cannot be found because it is not a thing that has been lost.

The sentient being called human is constantly teetering on the edge of self-realization. If one can only let go of all need for control and efforts of becoming, the realization arises.

NOVEMBER

1ˢᵀ OF NOVEMBER

thought is like a flower. Every time a thought arises, it is encircled by relationships to other thoughts. It is beautiful in its illusoriness.

2ᴺᴰ OF NOVEMBER

The road is slippery. Much care must be taken while driving the car toward the office. The rain of supercooled water during the small hours has created a treacherous blanket of dense ice on the asphalt. Testing the brakes of the car results in a very slow deceleration, as the tire studs try to sink into the icy surface.

Already late from an important meeting at work, and even though a considerable problem is perceived in being late, no problem is experienced. A strong desire to see and experience a problem in the situation is present in the mind, but in compassionate awareness, it is rendered meaningless.

Any desire is a seed of suffering. Whenever one desires something, resistance against the present moment arises. Whenever a desire is ignored or avoided, its looming presence stays in the background. Whenever a desire is fulfilled, it will grow stronger. The nature of desire is imprisonment. One cannot get rid of desires, and even desiring so is a similar kind of desire as any other desire. Only realizing the impossibility of breaking out of the imprisonment of desires breaks the chains.

3ᴿᴰ OF NOVEMBER

It has been raining most of the day, and the weather is quite warm again. The rain pounds the roof of the house and the darkness outside is very tangible. The window is like a dark painting, depicting mostly impenetrable blackness accompanied by a few gloomy silhouettes of the trees.

Staring at the next empty passage of *A Year of Stillness* like so many times before. The bright light of the computer screen creates a deep contrast with the darkness emanating from the window. Whatever has led to the situation of sitting and staring at the empty space on the page is covered in darkness. But what matters is that the empty space needs to be filled at this very moment.

The purpose of writing this text escapes the understanding—the reasons for it are hidden. Nevertheless, writing happens when it happens. If it does not, the space for the day is left empty. The writing is never coerced, as nothing in life should be. Force always creates resistance, and suffering follows in the wake of resistance.

The year is soon coming to an end, but no hurry is experienced in the process of the writing. The topics for each day seem to have a life of their own, and they flow through the stillness of just being. Sometimes they flow entirely out of reach, and then nothing comes out. Sometimes they are hazy like a dream and need some contemplation to put in words. Sometimes they are clear as a cloudless sky, and the text for the day is already written before even opening the text for writing.

5TH OF NOVEMBER

While in the middle of eating breakfast and drifting in a stream of unnecessary thinking, the daughters suddenly ask the questions: "Where has everything come from? What is God?" The mind and the body stop, and the answer arises first as a formless sense of being, and then it gradually starts to emerge as words.

God is all that is. Nothing exists that is not God. Even calling something 'God' is God expressing itself through a simple word. It is not separate from anything and connected to *everything* that exists, as well as to that which does *not* exist. It is all that is seen, as well as the great unseen. It is acceptance and rejection at the same time. Atheism is God expressing itself through atheistic beliefs and actions. Religion is God expressing itself through religious beliefs and actions. It covers all aspects of what is called life—it is life.

God is both the child asking "What is God?" and the parent explaining what God is. God is in everything observed and unobserved. Its nature is too paradoxical for the mind to understand, yet it is the simplest thing—or nothing—that could exist. Anything that is experienced as God is only an insignificantly minor part of God, yet it exists in the smallest detail of existence as a whole. It cannot be pointed to, yet anywhere one points to cannot miss the presence of God.

God is the source of existence itself and whatever form it might take. It is the explanations of existence in whatever words it might be described. It has no beginning or ending, and its presence is undeniable everywhere and every time. God is the whispering of the stillness within every single part of itself. It is the silent presence and the liveliness of life. It holds sufferings and pleasures, and underneath them, it is the inevitable freedom of unchanging eternity. It is peace, and it is love, but not in any way the mind could comprehend. The peace and love God holds within are unconditional.

Before all, God is in everyone's reach all the time. One has never parted from God, as it is not even possible. Any belief system one might carry about the existence of a god is an expression of God. The silent eternity of it all is revealed in just being still, and getting out of one's own way. When the spirit is blown empty of all false ideas and concepts of oneself, God will show up.

6TH OF NOVEMBER

Soft drizzle caresses the face while walking on the street. The morning is still early, and only a few others are seen. The people passing by seem to be curled up inside themselves, and the expressions of their faces indicate some heavy thinking. Their posture and the pace of their walking echo of an invisible dream. Full of thoughts, people drift to anywhere their patterns of thinking are taking them. They cannot see the world because they are standing in front of it themselves.

The world is seen entirely when one gets out of one's own way. Focusing the awareness on external things while being aware of the act of focusing is one of the portals to inner peace. Inner peace can never exist as long as anything exists inside. Peace is revealed only by the absence of things. As one's undivided attention consciously shifts to the external world, emptiness is revealed within. It is not the emptiness of the mind, but true emptiness, which means no one is there. It cannot even be an object of awareness. In this emptiness, the illusory nature of the ego and any 'I'-related thoughts become clear.

Holding on to the false identity of oneself is like holding one's breath. It is forced, and it depletes energy. Only when one exhales, and no air is left in the lungs, new air can get in through inhaling. The fresh air always holds the potential for healing. An inner vacuum must be created to really invite the world to step in. No place for any kind of divine being exists, if one stubbornly holds on to an illusory image of oneself.

The soft drizzle keeps on falling down from the dark sky. The footsteps are clearly heard, and the hard surface of the asphalt creates a peaceful sensation in the soles. Everything drifts through a bottomless and objectless sense of stillness.

7TH OF NOVEMBER

A control paradox arises in inner stillness. As one merges with the inner stillness, a deep sense of oneness is felt, and one becomes the surrounding world. One becomes the awareness of the world, without any sense of identity clinging to the things in the world. In a world created by oneself, control is magnificent and unrivaled, yet a certain touch of totally losing the control arises. At the same time, one is in control of everything and yet nothing.

The greatest expression of free will is the act of stepping back from what is called life, and just being aware of everything that happens. No free will exists, if one does not first step out of one's own mind. While stepping back, there can be no control of life and one's own actions. The seed of all control and true free will is planted only when one dares to let go of all control and any thoughts of free will.

Allowing life to have its own way without any personal interference is painful, and from the viewpoint of the mind, highly illogical. However, from the act of letting go of control emerges an ability to continuously acquire true control of one's own life. The control paradox withholds a magnificent and beautiful symmetry, in which no force needs to be exercised to have control of life. After all, there is no one controlling the life, and no identity pulling the strings. Life takes care of itself, and aligning with life is the way to shatter all illusions.

8TH OF NOVEMBER

It is amazing how quickly the darkness withdraws in the morning and comes in when the evening arrives. The daily moments of brightness are quite short, and the light of the day silently wanes into the darkness of the night in their never-ending playful dance.

The lack of snow deepens the darkness making it an impenetrable black wall before the eyes. The sounds of the sea are heard clearly as the waves hit the beach, but nothing is seen in the darkness embracing the sea. The scent of the forest of autumn is subtle, and the noise of the trees swaying in the gentle breeze whispers wordless words. The sky is not visible, and only bottomless darkness hovers above. Everything embraced by the darkness remains a strange, yet familiar mystery.

14TH OF NOVEMBER

Several days have passed in an incessant stream of thinking. Moments of clarity have arisen here and there, but they have not lasted as the mind quickly grasps them, turning them into spiritual symbols and intellectual arrogance. However, something has changed so subtly that one would not be aware of it without the habit of relentless inquiry into one's own thoughts. What has changed, is that the thoughts bear no such importance anymore as they used to. They still pour in like rainfall from the grey sky, but identification with the thoughts is not so deep as it has been in the past.

As thoughts lose their importance, the relationship with oneself silently disintegrates. It feels joyful and mysteriously peaceful. No greater freedom exists than to be free of the 'I' within, that dwells in all the myriad mental positions, beliefs, and ten thousand different habits of resistance. Even though thinking happens compulsively, and the thoughts come in practically unceasingly, the awareness of them breathes somewhere in the background. Being aware of thoughts means letting go of the control one believes to have over the thoughts.

The familiar stillness and peacefulness within deepen when the feeling of control is relinquished. Just like the greatest freedom is found in the disintegration of the relationship with oneself, the greatest control over life can be acquired only by giving up the need for control. All need for control is a by-product of the false identity, which thrives off of inner resistance.

The rain falls down from the gloomy sky, yet a deep peacefulness is felt within its constant embrace. The silence is deep. The stillness prevails.

15TH OF NOVEMBER

Lots of householding tasks are needed this evening. Myriad little things and toys lie in places they shouldn't, the plants need watering, the new training room has to be painted, and the whole house is in desperate need of vacuuming. One task at a time, the house gets into order again as the whole family carries out their responsibilities in the cleaning. Even the daughters are motivated to clean, even though many times they are distracted by some beloved toy or a spontaneous play of some kind.

No heaviness is felt while doing ordinary tasks. A lightness of undefined joy arises while picking up some random toys off the floor. A wordless sense of an idea lingers on top of the mind:

This is all that exists, and in the next moment, this has already evaporated and merged with the nothingness from whence this all came.

Just like this very moment, life is fleeting. In a blink of an eye, this life is no more. It makes one understand how precious the present moment actually is. What could be more magnificent than to witness something existing now, when nothing else but utter emptiness embraces the '*now*'? There is nothing, that could rival the power of simple existence. Nothing that could threaten its precious essence.

However, to see the precious in the present moment, courage is needed to render all thoughts and all external things to unimportance. Nothing must be held important to see the magnificence of the moment, not even the most intimate relationships there might be. Paradoxically, through entirely relinquishing the importance held toward external things, all things gain a new and unrivaled feeling of importance—such that the human mind is unable to see. Unconditional importance. Non-judgmental importance.

Nothing embraces the present moment. Not even time, and especially not even some supernatural or godlike entity, nor a thing called enlightenment. Just being there, without anything to relate to and without an opposite, the present moment silently flows like a wave without an ocean. Its power is tremendous and compassionate.

17ᵀᴴ OF NOVEMBER

People always try to become something, to transcend something they are at the moment. Transcendence from something to something else is but a change of form, in which there can be no real transcendence. It is just shifting the consciousness to another state. Change of form happens even though one did not strive for it. Change happens inevitably as the world changes.

True transcendence is not from something to something else, but from nothing to something. Transcending from nothing to something is the power of existence itself and the endless wave of wordless becoming. As one blows out everything held within the mind and creates a vacuum inside, the world flows into one's being. Being and doing meet halfway on the path from non-existence to existence, and when this happens, anything one does will inevitably be beneficial to the world. And whatever is beneficial to the world, is beneficial to oneself with full certainty.

When nothing becomes something in the present moment, true transcendence is made manifest. No effort in the vicious loop of becoming accompanies it, as already being something is sufficient. This endless wave of existence is the basis of all that is, and it channels itself from the flipside of all that is; the nothingness which fulfills the infinite circle of the absolute.

21ST OF NOVEMBER

Ten thousand things arise in the street. Some Christmas lights are already hanging above the pedestrian street, and the light they emit is warm and welcoming. The street is full of people, moving to all possible directions. Some pigeons seek food and maneuver through the countless feet of the people. A group of children plays in front of the big granite sphere, the famous landmark in the heart of the city.

Life flourishes, and even though chaotic movement is experienced while strolling through the street, a deep peace embraces all movement. A profound stillness breathes inside the movement, forever inhaling and exhaling at the same time. It is a healing stillness, which holds the continuous cycle of destruction and creation within. And even the destruction and creation are but concepts in the still movement of existence.

22ND OF NOVEMBER

The full moon shines brightly in the dark sky. Occasionally, a few clouds roll by, obstructing the brightness for a short while. Whenever it happens, the otherwise dark silhouettes of the clouds are covered with bright silver outlines, and their shapes are illuminated in most mysterious ways. The view is pristine, and the moment whispers words of benediction and the endless compassion of the inner stillness.

Just like the clouds, some thoughts occasionally appear, and just like the clouds, whenever the thoughts appear, they are illuminated by the light of the awareness. The bright silver outlines of the thoughts are sensed almost physically. Full awareness of thoughts, and the mystery of the thoughts is there, deep and serene. It is the same mystery that embraces the whole existence, yet it is not a mystery to be solved in any way. The mystery of the inner stillness and everything that is perceived from the stillness is actually nothingness.

Nothing exists beyond the sense of the mystery. This makes the mystery of existence so magnificent. At the same time, it is something so intricate and unsolved, that the mind cannot even start to grasp it, and yet it is so peaceful, that the mind does not even hold a desire to grasp it. There is no far side to the extent of our knowledge, but only peaceful nothingness. Whatever mystery we meet at the outermost reaches of our knowledge, is not a mystery at all, even though a sense of mystery is prone to arise.

The moon illuminates the darkness of the night with the beautiful and all-encompassing light. The far side of the full moon breathes deep inner stillness through its unseen nature.

26ᵀᴴ OF NOVEMBER

The moon shines faintly through the hazy layer of clouds. The darkness of winter is heavy on the morning, and the freezing cold feels crisp and clean while inhaling. No snow covers the ground yet, but everything is covered in white frost. The coldness of winter is soothing, as it resembles the inner peace that's available at any given moment.

When it is cold, nature is altogether still. Very little movement is seen. Whatever moves seems like its movement was slowed down, and the movement is somehow curled within itself. All the sounds are curiously covered by a deep silence, and whenever sounds are observed, they seem very distinct and alive. The effervescence of existence sleeps in the embrace of the winter's coldness, and anything that arises from the coldness is vividly alive.

In the false identity, existence is afraid of itself. It is a state of constant denial, embraced by a deep urge for becoming. But it is a necessity, and finding this state of denial and fear in oneself is one of the most distinct pathways to liberation. The state of denial and fear is there only because without it, one could never become aware of the limitless state of inner love, openness, and allowance. Being aware of all those attributes of existence, no need to become anything arises. Just being the awareness is perfectly sufficient.

28TH OF NOVEMBER

One can never know what layers of identity the world reveals in the next moment. The identities of future moments are as unknown as the future is. There might be clues and guesses about it, creating an illusion of preparation, but the true nature of the next moment cannot be experienced '*here and now*' yet. Only the state of preparation can be experienced when preparing for any future moment.

The future moment can be experienced only when the moment arrives, and the only truth carried into that moment is the awareness of the moment, and the awareness of oneself. The false identity is always shaped by the external circumstances of the moment, but the self, which is aware of it all, stays the same. The *self* is unchanging.

29TH OF NOVEMBER

Life between the two great unknowns seems very small. In that smallness, all the memories and expectations are rendered meaningless. They still arise from moment to moment, but their significance is not defining life in any way. The great unknown that embraces the present moment is very tangible but seen only when the veil of thinking evaporates.

Something breathes in the present moment, and it cannot really be defined what it is—at least not through the tools of the mind. And needless to say, it is impossible through written words. It is a sense of impeccable and inevitable something, that constantly arises within the core of one's own being. It shines its light on all the surface phenomena that one calls experiences.

In the moments of inner stillness, this something is more evident than anything could ever be. In the moments of inner whirlwinds of thinking, its light is suppressed. But even when suppressed, it is still there somewhere beneath everything. The peaceful state of unknowing is the essence of it.

The unknown nature of the light makes the present moment, where all the knowledge resides, almost painfully distinct and significant. Nothing is more important in what is called life than the presence of each and every moment.

DECEMBER

2ND OF DECEMBER

The sunrise paints the cloudy sky bright orange. The wave-like surface of the bottom of the clouds shines like thousands of embers, shedding the beautiful orange light on the dawn of the new day. A sense of inner stillness is present, reflecting externally in the peace of the unmoving layer of orange clouds.

Light is the foundation of existence. Where there is no light, an experience of the absence of light arises, connecting intrinsically to the existence of the light. Even if one were blind, and had no concept of light to contemplate, the light would still be there, in many different forms and a multitude of experiences. The visible light is only one of the forms of light, just as the individual experience is only one form of existence. Through myriad forms, the formless is seen, and the forms of light become the essence of light.

In the essence of light, all forms arise and fall, like the orange embers shine for their time on the surface of the clouds. All forms appear from the essence and wither away into the same source from whence they came. There is no form in existence that could be separate from this ongoing process of appearance and disappearance because existence is an expression of this process.

The process cannot be seen as it is the great unseen. It can be sensed indirectly through an unrivaled sense of inner peace and stillness, but even that sensation is not it. The process is felt in the unexplainable joy of doing different things, especially routine and minor things in one's life. It is felt as a joy without a particular reason, but it is not that joy. The closest thing for the process is the awareness through which one perceives the world in the state of inner peace, stillness, and joy. This awareness is of a creation that appreciates whatever has been created.

3RD OF DECEMBER

The ground is covered in fresh white snow. The landscape looks profoundly different than yesterday, and it feels like a totally different world was created this morning. Nature seems renewed and adapted to the white blanket of soft snow. Everything is new and beautiful.

Despite the change in the surrounding world, something within stays the same. Something is aware of all the changes, just like it has always been before, and will always be after. It is the awareness, the essence of life, which cannot be stained by changes in any way. The essence remains as it ever was. It cannot wear out because it was never produced. It cannot perish because it was never created. Ultimately, it cannot even *be* because it *never was*.

Despite this, the essence is '*here and now*'. In every grain of awareness, there is a center, that seems to be everywhere at the same time. It cannot be divided by space or time. Whatever the vantage point in existence is, the point is experienced as the center of existence. Realizing this is the way to pure and sincere compassion. In the embrace of unlimited compassion, existence whispers to itself in every single relationship that happens:

You are just like you, as I am me. Together, we are.

10TH OF DECEMBER

A sense of mental relaxation is very present this morning. Only a few thoughts flow by here and there, and mostly when deciding to think. The perception is directed outward, instead of inner mental positions and the false sense of identity.

The ground is covered with slush, and wet snow is falling down from the dark sky above. The air feels damp. The weather could be described as dismal, but there is nothing dismal about the world this morning—just inner peace and silence.

The familiar stillness within prevails and the darkness of the morning seems to amplify the feeling of it. As the perception is purely directed outward, no sense of identity seems to be present. All illusions have evaporated in this present moment. The world seems vividly alive. Lots of movement happens everywhere, and in that movement, the deep and wordless meaning of everything is felt very distinctly. Nothing can describe this meaning but the direct and pure experience of it.

The stillness within is brought by the perception of external movement, and it has loosened all tension in the state of being. When the false identity is active, it is always accompanied by a curious kind of mental tension. It happens even when there is seemingly no negative thinking occurring. The tension of the mind is still there, even when everything seems fine. Many times that tension also reflects in the body through uneasiness and unconscious tension in the muscles.

Inner and outer peace is felt when the tension is released through the power of the present moment. In the present moment, the direct perception of *all* things makes the false identity evaporate, and at the same time, all need for any kind of control disappears as well. As the need for control does not arise anymore, one is at peace with oneself and with the world. A deep state of acceptance and trust arises.

11TH OF DECEMBER

The source of existence is in plain sight, yet it is so subtle that it cannot be noticed as long as the awareness identifies with the myriad things in its existence. It cannot be realized in the chamber of echoes called 'the mind'. Even the mind's best efforts and deepest contemplations can only scratch the surface of the source. The realization of the source can happen only through pure experience, where there is no mind involved in shaping the perceived reality. The act of perception must be unstained.

One must remove *everything* to find out the only thing that cannot be removed. Ultimately, this thing is not even a thing. What is no-thing cannot be an object of awareness. After removing all illusions, it becomes evident that one cannot be aware of oneself as an object of awareness, and through this evidence, the source is realized.

12TH OF DECEMBER

To see reality, one must learn to love the present moment more than the illusory mind-made reality. There must be a desire to love the present moment, but the desire cannot arise as long as a false sense of identity is derived from the mind. The mind can express love, but only a clinging and grasping kind of love, which is temporary at best. There are moments of loving, and moments of not loving, and in that pendulum of loving and not loving the mind blindly struggles. The love created by the human mind has fragile foundations.

The desire to love, to purely and sincerely love, can be acquired only through relentless and continuous observation of oneself. The act of awareness reveals what one is not, and then a new sense of self begins to surface. It is always fresh and new, yet it has always been. The awareness of oneself must become the state of being one defaults to. Only then is the true desire to love the present moment revealed and the love of the present moment exceeds thousandfold the love of the mind-made reality.

However, acquiring the desire to love the present moment is not a road that must be traveled through time, but only an aspect of life that becomes revealed as it ever was. No steps must be taken on that road to realizing love, but sometimes one needs the many steps to realize that no steps are required.

18TH OF DECEMBER

The unusually long flu is taking its toll on the body. Every day, the body feels weary after work. Not much energy is left for writing. Despite the weariness, the mind holds some pressure for the writing process, and it whispers stressful words: "The last month should be full of text and important messages. It is the *grand finale* of the year. You should write! Force yourself to write!"

A subtle kind of compassion is always felt when the mind starts whispering its many words—sincere compassion. It arises without any thoughts of compassion, and it always becomes revealed at the same time when the mind begins ranting about things. This compassion fosters sincerity toward the process of writing. The writing happens only through the cessation of all identity-related mind activity. It is not forced in any way, and it is as it should be.

The end of the year is arriving fast. The soothing darkness of the fleeting days is long.

19ᵀᴴ OF DECEMBER

The awareness has become a safe haven—a default state of being. Occasionally, drifting off to the oblivion of compulsive thinking happens, only to return to the center, to the *'here and now'*. The awareness of the present moment turns the mental interpretation of things into things as they are. Without effort. With fulfillment.

20ᵀᴴ OF DECEMBER

The heavy snow weighs down the branches of the trees. The forest seems to be in a deep immovable slumber. Everything is tranquil and peaceful. The whole view of the landscape indistinctly points downward as if nature itself was sleeping. Some light snowflakes hover in the air. A small bird flies by. Silently and elegantly it lands on a branch of a nearby tree.

The field of time seems to slow down when awareness arises. Ultimately, with enough recognition of the awareness, the experience of time disappears totally. This does not mean that one's own form as a human being would be taken out of the realm of time, but the timeless dimension of being affects the form, eventually reaching the thoughts and actions.

No fear of death appears in the timeless dimension of being. When there is no fear of death, there is unlimited compassion for every single form appearing in time. All of them shine the most beautiful light for their time and then fade into the world like the snowflakes merge into the white snow-covered ground.

22ND OF DECEMBER

The full moon illuminates the night. Everything bathes in its beautiful and subtle rays of light. The night holds even more light than an average day during this time of winter. The moon is unusually bright. The crisp and cold air feels refreshing in the lungs and throat, as the body is just recovering from the long flu. The snow glimmers in the moonlight like there were thousands of little diamonds scattered on its surface. The blue light of the moon breathes in harmony with the coldness of the air.

Many times, a busy and stressful mind longs for peace, but the peace that is longed for, or is even temporarily attained, is but a mere expression of the busy and stressful mind. That kind of peace has nothing to do with true inner peace. However, true inner peace is attainable through recognizing, accepting, and observing the busy and stressful mind. Any effort to change the state of the mind is one of the many gateways to illusions.

A whole world of illusions lingers in the depths of the mind. When pure awareness arises through accepting the present state of mind, only one question remains:

If the whole world is an illusion, then who is the illusionist?

26TH OF DECEMBER

The moon is bright in the midday's light blue sky. The sun shines somewhere behind the forest, creating a distinct line on the icy surface of the sea where the shadow meets the light. In the shadow, the sea ice is deep white in a monotonous color. In the light, the shadows and bright orange hues of light share an elegant dance as the light reflects from the wave-like icy surface of the sea.

The dance is immovable, yet all its details are countless. Whatever is perceived, the details are different. Every form created by the light and shadows is unique in every possible way. However, they share something in common—not in their form, but in the act of perception. One can see oneself in all those forms. Perception is what gives life to experience, and the perception of experience creates an opening into the formless dimension within oneself.

In this dimension, forms arise and fall, dancing like the light and shadows on the surface of the icy sea. Every form is unique, yet perceived from the same mutual vantage point. This point is everywhere and every time. It covers everything in existence—it is one.

Forms are always different. Their consequences are many. But on the formless level of existence, one lives in all sentient beings through the sense of the *self*, the center within. It is the same in all because it is one, undivided, undefinable, everything and nothing, and without an opposite.

Forms and things are surface phenomena. They happen within the essence of awareness, and they cannot define the essence in any way. Nevertheless, they are a significant part of realizing the essence. Because of this, all forms should be appreciated and accepted as they are.

27TH OF DECEMBER

A thick fog covers the sea. The vast blanket of snow on the icy sea merges with the fog, creating an impenetrable wall of whiteness. In that whiteness, there are no objects that can be perceived—no things, no animals, and no horizon. Nothing, but pure and pristine white. It is accompanied by deep silence of the surrounding nature. The absence of noise is peaceful.

In the absence of perceivable things, no experience arises. Occasionally, the mind tries to create an illusory experience, but as soon as it arises, the awareness embraces the experience. In its futile efforts in creating a false world, the mind falls silent.

An infinite number of worlds linger in the fog beyond perception. They cannot be known as long as they are not perceived. Any knowledge that is not a result of pure and direct experience is knowledge brought by the mind. Such knowledge is illusory, and experiences triggered by such knowledge are illusory as well.

There are many worlds unknown. In them, lies the undefinable potential of all that is.

28TH OF DECEMBER

Foxfires. The dance of the light in the pitch black sky brings forth a sense of mystery. If the light had a voice, it would sing wordless songs about the forests of the night, and it would praise the silent coldness embracing the snow-covered nature. In that coldness lies the craving for the experience of warmth, just like the perception of the bright foxfires tells a story about the unending blackness of space. The world of forms is a world of opposites, which can never exist without one another.

The wordless understanding of aware presence unveils a sense of loneliness within one's being. Not many are ready for such an understanding. However, the loneliness arises simultaneously with a fulfilling experience of peaceful solitude. Through solitude, oneness emerges. It climbs ever upwards from the shadows of the unseen valleys of existence, adapting distinct forms of fells and mountains. Somewhere far beyond it all, yet impossibly near, silent *being* breathes. It inhales and exhales at the same time, with a never-ending rhythm.

    Peacefully and lovingly.

    Compassionately.

    Gratefully.

JANUARY

1ST OF JANUARY

The first day of a new year dawns in soothing darkness, and after everything, I still am.

Made in the USA
Coppell, TX
20 January 2021